THE
GREAT COMPOSERS
THEIR LIVES AND TIMES

Béla
Bartók
1881-1945

Igor
Stravinsky
1882-1971

Carl
Orff
1895-1982

George
Gershwin
1898-1937

THE GREAT COMPOSERS
THEIR LIVES AND TIMES

Béla

Bartók

1881-1945

Igor

Stravinsky

1882-1971

Carl

Orff

1895-1982

George

Gershwin

1898-1937

MARSHALL CAVENDISH
NEW YORK · LONDON · SYDNEY

Staff Credits

Editors
Laura Buller
David Buxton

Art Editors
Helen James
Debbie Jecock

Deputy Editor
Barbara Segall

Sub-editors
Geraldine Jones
Judy Oliver
Nigel Rodgers

Designers
Steve Chilcott
Shirin Patel
Chris Rathbone

Picture Researchers
Georgina Barker
Julia Calloway
Vanessa Cawley

Production Controllers
Deborah Cracknell
Sue Fuller

Secretary
Lynn Small

Publishing Director
Reg Wright

Managing Editor
Sue Lyon

Consultants
Dr Antony Hopkins
Commander of the Order
of the British Empire
Fellow of the
Royal College of Music

Nick Mapstone BA, MA

Keith Shadwick BA

Reference Edition Published 1990

Published by Marshall Cavendish Corporation
147 West Merrick Road
Freeport, Long Island
N.Y. 11520

Typeset by Maclink, Hull
Printed by Times Offset Private Ltd.,
Singapore

© *Marshall Cavendish Limited MCMLXXXIV,*
MCMLXXXVII, MCMXC

Library of Congress Cataloging-in-Publication Data

The Composers: the great composers, their lives and times.
  p. ca.
    Cover title: Great composers II.
    ISBN 1-85435-300-4 (set): $175.00
    1. Composers—Biography.   2. Music appreciation.
I. Marshall Cavendish Corporation.
II. Title: Great composers II.
ML390.C7185 1990   780'.92'2—dc20 [B]   89-23988

ISBN 1-85435-300-4 (set)   *CIP*
  1-85435-305-5 (vol)   *MN*

THE
GREAT COMPOSERS
THEIR LIVES AND TIMES

Contents

Introduction

From the Renaissance period onwards, orchestral music was dominated by regular patterns in its construction. Traditions in melodic progression, harmonics, structure and the major and minor key systems were developed and, in general, adhered to by the following generations of composers. But the early 20th century saw many new musical approaches. Composers experimented with revolutionary styles, new sound colours, different scales and complex rhythm structures. The four composers in this volume were part of this wave of experimentation, and the revolutionary works they created laid a firm foundation for modern music.

Béla Bartók collected folk music from his native Hungary; in his compositions, he evoked its insistent rhythms and complex tonalities. Yet

Bartók reshaped folk elements to express his own personal vision, creating an intensely modern style of music. Igor Stravinsky is now acknowledged as the giant of 20th century music. Shifting the emphasis from the string section to the percussion and wind sections, he created a bold, powerful style which has become characteristic of much modern music. Carl Orff was not only a composer of spectacularly dramatic works, but an innovator in the field of music education for children. He felt that music was the unity of sound, language and movement; he used these elements to create simple yet powerful music.

George Gershwin took a taste of jazz into the concert hall with his stunning works. The strength of his melodies and the syncopated rhythms he borrowed from jazz forms give his music great power and vitality.

THE GREAT COMPOSERS

Béla Bartók

1881–1945

Béla Bartók was perhaps Hungary's greatest composer, and his legacy of works is undisputably among the finest compositions of the early 20th century. His exhaustive study of the folk music of Hungary and eastern Europe had a profound effect on his compositions, yet his understanding of contemporary music helped him to create his homogeneous, highly personal style. His works emphasized energetic rhythms, folk melodies and vivid dissonances; his use of brash, jarring chords caused much controversy. But today he is much admired for his works, which include the Concerto for Orchestra and the Dance Suite, both analysed in the Listener's Guide. *These passionate, complex compositions show a startling newness in technique; artists in Bartók's time were developing equally startling new movements and* In The Background *describes the origins of modern art.*

8

The young Bartók showed such promise as a pianist and composer that his teachers at the Budapest Academy of Music waived his final exams. Dividing his time between academic work at the Academy, composing and gathering folk songs throughout Hungary, Bartók soon consolidated his compositional progress with a series of remarkable works. Orchestras called his music unplayable and critics described it as tonal chaos, yet Bartók soon found an audience with a successful tour of Europe in 1922. Over the following years, he toured the United States and Russia as his reputation as both a composer and as a musicologist grew. In 1940, he left his troubled homeland of Hungary for the last time to take up exile in America. Although he immersed himself in his work, his achievements were largely overlooked; tragically, it was not until after his death in New York in 1945 that his works found a firm place in the 20th-century musical repertoire.

Interfoto MTI/Boosey and Hawkes

COMPOSER'S LIFE

'Tonal chaos'

Neglected, misunderstood and even notorious during his lifetime, Béla Bartók was hailed internationally as one of the most popular modern composers within a few years of his death.

Hungary's indigenous music, history and traditions were rooted deep in the countryside (left) and exerted a powerful and early influence on Bartók who was born into an agricultural community.

After the death of Bartók's father the family moved home several times as his mother sought to find work for herself and a good education for her children. Bartók was eventually enrolled, in 1899, at the Budapest Academy of Music (below).

Béla Bartók was born in the small town of Nagyzentmiklós in South-East Hungary on 25 March 1881. He was born into a musical family: his mother, formerly a teacher, was a particularly gifted pianist and his father, headmaster of the agricultural school, was also a talented cello player.

Béla's interest in music was evident very early on and by the age of five he had begun piano lessons. In 1888, when he was seven, his father died after a short illness, aged only 33. Bartók's mother, Paula, in order to support her family, was forced to resume the teaching career she had abandoned on her marriage. Bartók's musical ability continued to mature and his mother was determined to see it properly nurtured by first-rate teachers. Accordingly, she took leave of absence from her school in 1892 and removed the family to Pozsony (now Bratislava) where she hoped to find a new post. When, at the end of her year's absence, she had not found anything suitable she was transferred to a post at Beszterce where, although she found work, there was no suitable music teacher for Bartók. In April 1894 the family returned once more to Pozsony where Paula found a job at a teacher-training college and Béla settled down to five years of uninterrupted musical studies at the Pozsony Gymnasium (high school).

Musical student in Budapest

By 1899 Béla had completed his secondary schooling and it was decided, although he was offered a place at the Vienna Conservatoire, that he should continue his musical studies at the Budapest Academy of Music instead. During his first few months he was dogged by ill-health but he did finish the academic year successfully. However, he was unable to continue his studies in his second year due to a severe bout of pneumonia which he contracted in August 1901. He recuperated at home with his

mother for several months before resuming his studies in April 1901. He had been a frail sickly child and ill-health was to recur throughout his student years.

During his years at the Academy Bartók's musical horizons were increasingly widened but it was after attending a première of *Also sprach Zarathustra* that he discovered the music of Strauss, which was to renew in him his earlier interest and enthusiasm for composition. His first compositions – waltzes and polkas – were produced when he was nine. A few years later aged 11, he had made his début as performer and composer with *The course of the Danube*. The influence of Strauss's music unleashed a creativity which had not been stirred by the traditional techniques of the Academy.

Bartók completed his studies at the Academy in June 1903. His teachers saw him as a pianist with a

In 1905 Bartók went to Paris to compete for the Prix Rubinstein – a prize open to gifted young pianists. Although he was disappointed in the outcome – he came second – and there were one or two clashes over the 'performability' of his music', he enjoyed being in Paris. He was particularly taken with the night-life and character of the cabarets and bars of seamy Montmartre (right).

brilliant career ahead of him and he was given the opportunity to perform at many Academy concerts, where he played some of his own earlier compositions. Such was his talent as both a pianist and composer that the final examination at the Academy was waived: 'the general opinion is that this is superfluous', he related in a letter to his mother.

In the winter of 1903 Bartók moved around Europe and achieved recognition as a composer with his symphonic poem *Kossuth,* which was premièred in Budapest and Manchester, and the *Violin Sonata.* He also established a reputation as a performer, playing his own and other people's compositions at concerts in Budapest, Vienna and Pozsony.

The inspiration of folk songs

From April 1904 he spent several months staying with his sister in the Hungarian countryside. It was here that, quite by chance, he first heard authentic Hungarian folk music, sung by a local girl in the village. After his return from Paris where, in 1905, he had competed for the Rubinstein Prize, Bartók began organizing his first information-gathering tour

While he was at school in Pozsony Bartók met the son of one of his teachers, Ernö von Dohnányi (left), who was to become a lifelong friend. Dohnányi, later to become a distinguished composer himself, had a considerable influence on Bartók's taste and ideas during his early musical development.

BBC Hulton Picture Library

around Hungary. 'As I went from village to village', he later wrote, 'I heard the true music of my race . . . This music was a revelation to me . . .' Before this journey he made contact with Zoltan Kodály, a composer and expert on the study of folk song.

Both men, destined to be great composers in their own right, originally looked upon this material as a source of inspiration for their own compositions. But over many trips in the next few years their prime concern became the preservation and study of the music itself. The first fruits of this work were co-authored and published in 1906 as *Twenty Hungarian Folksongs.*

The following year, in January 1907, Bartók was appointed to the staff of the Budapest Academy of Music, taking the position of teacher of the advanced piano class. In the two years leading to this appointment, he had been so occupied with his research into and collection of folk music that he had composed nothing of his own. With his interests drifting ever further from a concert career, the Academy post was both a vocational and financial godsend.

During 1907 he embarked on an intense relationship with a girl seven years younger than himself, the virtuoso violinist Stefi Geyer. The affair was doomed from the start, Stefi being a devout Catholic whereas Bartók was an atheist. The strain of trying to accommodate such opposite views eventually destroyed the relationship, but not before they had exchanged a series of deeply-felt letters, and Bartók had written some remarkable compositions, including the first *Violin Concerto* and the *Two Portraits (The Ideal* and *The Grotesque),* especially for Stefi.

Marriage to Márta

It was in the emotional aftermath of their affair that Bartók met his future wife. Called Márta Ziegler, she was just fourteen when they met (Bartók was 26). Within a few months of their meeting they had become greatly attracted to each other, and in 1908 Bartók made his first dedication to her, a little piano piece called *Picture of a Girl.*

The events of these years had given a new emotional maturity to Bartók, both in his life and in his work. His orchestral pieces found a wider audience throughout Europe, causing controversy at every turn. Many critics heard in his works only tonal chaos, and for much of his career he found himself either neglected or notorious as a composer of brash atonal music.

In 1909, at a simple and very private wedding, Bartók and the 16-year-old Márta were married. After the upheavals of the preceding years, Bartók's life finally took a more ordered turn. Márta gave birth to a son, also named Béla, in 1910.

Bartók continued with his work at the Academy and further consolidated his compositional progress. The following year, 1912, saw the completion of his only opera, *Duke Bluebeard's Castle,* which reflects the high-water mark of Debussy's influence on his work. By the end of 1912 both he and Kodály were at the receiving end of rough treatment from both critics and the public. As a result Bartók gave up all public musical activity and threw himself wholly into his folk researches. By the end of 1913 he had travelled through all of Hungary, parts of Romania, Transylvania and parts of North Africa. His articles on these researches were published all over the world and still stand today as models of careful research.

All this activity was abruptly curtailed in 1914 by Hungary's entry into World War I on the side of Austria. Bartók hated the war and lamented Hungary's involvement, seeing disaster as the only possible outcome. Luckily for him, he was found unfit for military service, and remained at the Academy for the duration of the war.

Renewal of activity

One indirect benefit of the war for him was an apparent renewal of his creativity, for, apart from the scholarly *Romanian Folksong Arrangements,* he completed the *Piano Suite Op. 14,* the second *String Quartet* and the ballet *The Wooden Prince* in the next three years. In 1917, against great opposition, the Italian conductor Egisto Tango brought *The Wooden Prince* to its Budapest première. He put his heart and soul into the production, defeating every sabotage attempt by the dancers and orchestra who had all pronounced it undanceable and unplayable before

Aus Ungarn

Tihany mit dem Balaton See

Bartók's desire to find the 'real' spirit of his homeland's people and music led him on a series of travels, after 1904, all over rural Hungary (left). What he discovered of the land, its people and music contrasted sharply with the Romantic notion of Hungary (above), as expressed in the music of composers such as Brahms and Liszt.

giving it a chance, and brought off a great success. Bartók remained eternally grateful to Tango who, the following year, also mounted the première of *Duke Bluebeard's Castle,* seven years after it was written. Bartók dedicated *The Wooden Prince* to him in appreciation of his effort.

The period after the end of the war brought increasing chaos and suffering to an already exhausted Hungary. Although both Bartók and Kodály were made Deputy Directors of the Academy under the new Provisional Government in 1919, the worsening political situation left no-one safe from the turmoil. At one point during the darkest days of Béla Kun's Communist terror, Béla and Márta were forced to flee their Budapest home, taking as many of their possessions as they could carry. When the Communists were overthrown and a rigidly conservative government installed, everyone feared for the positions given them by the former regime. Bartók survived, but Dohnányi, who had been Director, was removed. Kodály knew that he was a possible target, but his rigorously non-political public stance saved him from any reprisals.

Despite the turmoil, Bartok completed two *Sonatas for Violin and Piano,* and in 1922 he embarked on a highly successful concert tour of England, France, Germany and Italy, where the First Sonata in particular was given a warm reception, and his superlative piano playing was commented upon by many observers.

Before he set off on the tour he was beset by emotional problems. His marriage to Márta was fast disintegrating. In 1921 he had met his future second wife, Ditta Pásztory, in circumstances identical to his meeting of Márta: she came to him as a 19-year-old student and, as did most female students, developed a 'crush' on this handsome, quiet tutor and was thrilled to find her passion reciprocated. It is not known whether Bartók's marriage was in trouble before this; nor is it known why the marriage didn't survive the advent of Ditta. Strangely, when the split came in 1923, it was Márta who suggested a divorce so that Béla could marry Ditta. After a period of separation he and Márta met in August of that year to agree on the details.

The whole resolution of this episode was curiously painless, and after the marriage Márta remained a friend and was a frequent visitor to the new Bartók household. Ditta was 21, Bartók 41, when they married. Within a year she gave birth to a son, Peter. At the same time the contented Bartók returned to orchestral composition and produced the joyful *Dance Suite* – today one of his most popular pieces.

For the following few years Bartók's life settled into a welcome pattern of hard work and consistent inspiration in both his academic and creative fields. Piano pieces such as the *Sonata* (1926) and the *Out of Doors Suite* (1926) proved to be the equal of anything he had yet achieved, and the publication in 1924 of a book based on his researches, *Hungarian Folksong,* met with universal acclaim. In addition, Bartók kept up his concert-tour commitments, being well-received in both Italy and at the International Festival in Prague in 1925, where the *Dance Suite,* in particular, was a great success.

In 1927 a tour of the United States was arranged. Bartók managed sufficient leave from teaching to complete the long and arduous tour, but it was not

The title page, below, is from Bartók's piano pieces For Children. *This was first published in 1909 and was the result of one of his collecting tours of folk music in Slovakia and Romania.*

The Bettmann Archive Inc./BBC H.P.L.

Zoltan Kodály (left) was involved in similar folk research to Bartók. Together they revolutionized the study of folk music and between them collected thousands of folk songs. Many of these were recorded by Bartók on Edison cylinders (below).

Keystone

At the end of World War 1 Hungary was plunged into a period of political turmoil. During the worst days of terror inflicted by the communist government of Béla Kun many Hungarians were dispossessed and made homeless (right). At one point Béla and Márta Bartók fled from their Budapest home taking with them as many of their possessions as they could carry. It was some months before they returned to the city.

Bartók's only opera, **Duke Bluebeard's castle** *(set design below) was completed in 1912, but only given its première in Budapest in 1918. It was conducted by the Italian, Egisto Tango, who had conducted the première of Bartók's ballet,* **The Wooden Prince,** *so successfully in the previous year.*

Jean-Loup Charmet

nationalist aggression stemming from Germany and Italy during the 1930s. He made his point of view felt by refusing to include these countries in his concert tours or allowing his concerts to be broadcast there. Although intensely patriotic he found the blatant chauvinism and anti-semitism around him in Hungary impossible to condone. Yet while many of his colleagues all over Europe fled to America, Bartók remained in Budapest. Then, in 1938, Hitler entered Austria. The event was depressing enough in itself but it also meant that Bartók lost all his royalties since his publisher was in Austria and all payments were stopped by the Nazis.

Bartók could clearly foresee the takeover of Hungary by Germany, yet he was in a real quandary whether to stay or flee. He regarded exile as tantamount to artistic suicide, as so many of his creative links were with his own people. And there was also his mother to consider: he was adamant in his refusal to abandon her, and was committed to stay in Hungary while she was alive to prevent reprisals of any sort being taken against her.

War broke out in August 1939 and three months later his beloved mother died. In the light of these two events, he used his concert tour of America in early 1940 to sound out the possibility of migrating there. He found himself welcomed, and his tour with Hungarian expatriate violinist, Joseph Szigeti, was a real success. In October 1940, he and Ditta again left Hungary for America, officially to complete another concert tour, but all their friends knew the stay would be indefinite.

the success he had hoped for. Part of the reason was that he was just not the larger-than-life personality, either on or off stage, that the public takes to its heart. That he was simply a brilliant pianist and composer was not enough for the public at that time. His music was also 'difficult', and despite the support of such conductors as Mengelberg and Reiner, the reviews were hostile.

The tour was exhausting and Bartók was relieved to return to Hungary. However, the following year he entered his *Third String Quartet* in a Philadelphia competition and was rewarded with joint first prize.

Although in official music circles he received scant recognition at home, abroad his reputation grew not only as a performer and composer but also as a musicologist. He undertook a successful tour of Russia in 1929, playing to enthusiastic audiences in Kharkov, Odessa and Leningrad. In 1931 he was a guest at the Geneva Congress of Human Studies and that same year in honour of his 50th birthday he was made a Chevalier of the Legion of Honour in France. In an attempt to match this honour the Hungarian authorities awarded him the Corvin Wreath. However, because of his increasing disquiet over the fascist tendencies of the government, he declined to attend the ceremony.

For several years Bartók immersed himself in his researches and compositions. The result was a string of new works, including the brilliant *Second Piano Concerto,* and a major new publication in 1934 on Hungarian and neighbouring folk music. That same year he finally gave up teaching at the Academy. Along with his old friend Kodály he took up a research post offered by the Hungarian Academic Sciences to prepare for the publication of a folksong collection.

Though not actively involved in politics, Bartók became increasingly distressed by the mounting

Archiv für Kunst und Geschichte

The caricature (left) from a New York publication during Bartók's first visit to America in 1928 expresses the reception his 'difficult' music had there. One critic wrote that 'Bartók's music of last night is amoral, beyond good and evil, but hardly of Nietzschean expansiveness'.

In 1921 Bartók met Ditta Pásztory (left), then a 19-year-old student. Two years later his first wife, Márta, suggested a divorce and in August 1923 he and Ditta were married.

Exile in America

The story of Bartók's five years in America is a bleak and distressing one. Although he had regular employment on a small wage for the first two years at Columbia University in New York, his health was never good and his presence as a composer and concert artist was virtually ignored. At home he and Ditta feared for their son Peter's survival, as he was still in Hungary. Added to that, they were both desperately homesick and out of place in New York.

It is no surprise to find that Bartók attempted no creative work before 1942, but this did not mean that he was idle. With admirable practicality, he immersed himself in further research. Bartók had received a fellowship from Columbia University to work on the Milman Parry collection of Serbo-Croatian folk music at Harvard. Parry had made more than two thousand recordings mainly of epic songs in Yugoslavia. Bartók was assigned to transcribe and annotate the music, a task which obviously delighted him. On 25 November, 1940, he received an honorary doctorate from Columbia and although he was employed at a salary of $3000 per year he didn't feel secure, since the post was renewable each semester.

The personal pressures at least were eased in early 1942 when Béla and Ditta were reunited with their son, Peter, who had managed to reach the States through war-torn Europe. But although American friends continued to help Bartók find suitable work his music was still not being performed.

From April 1942 Bartók's health began to deteriorate rapidly. He suffered from high temperatures and weight loss – but for the time being, the leukemia which was to kill him remained undiagnosed. Despite his ill-health he struggled to find new work and on 21 January 1943 he gave his last concert performance. At the suggestion of one of his former pupils the American Society of Com-

posers, Authors and Publishers agreed to finance his medical treatment. At about the same time, secretly prompted by some of his friends who concealed all trace of what the independent-minded Bartók might see as charity, the conductor Serge Koussevitsky, commissioned him to compose an orchestral piece.

Though initially reluctant to start the work, Bartók finally flung himself into it and, as a startling rejection of the pain and desolation of his circumstances, he wrote the joyful and forward-looking *Concerto for Orchestra*.

By the end of the year he had met Yehudi Menuhin and accepted a commission from him for the *Solo Violin Sonata*. This was completed by early 1944, and premiered by Menuhin in New York later that year. That year saw an immense change in his composing fortunes, as commissions began to flow in, some of which he reluctantly turned down, concerned as he was with conserving his diminishing energies. One commission he did accept, from William Primrose, was for a *Viola Concerto*. But it was to remain unfinished at his death.

By this time it was clear to all that he was a dying man, although he himself refused to acknowledge it. He worked constantly on his third *Piano Concerto* and the *Viola Concerto*, fighting against a complete collapse of his health.

Peace in Europe brought with it news of his former wife, Márta, son Béla, and his friend and collaborator Kodály, all of whom had survived.

Bartók rested for most of the summer at Lake Saranac, working on his last two compositions, and was too ill to take up an invitation from the Menuhins to travel to California. By early September 1945 he had finished the draft of the *Viola Concerto* and the beautiful *Piano Concerto* was virtually completed. On his return to New York, however, his health finally gave way, and he spent his last few days in Mount Sinai Hospital and the West Side Hospital where he was transferred. He died on 26 September 1945. One of his last comments made to a hospital doctor sadly emphasizes his late period of creativity:

'I am only sorry that I have to leave with my baggage full.'

The final irony was that within the next few years he was to become one of the most internationally popular modern composers.

Orchestral works

In the 'Concerto for orchestra' and the 'Dance Suite', Bartók brilliantly developed the folk music of his native country to create a new but intensely personal musical language.

Short of money, in poor health and in exile from his homeland, Bartók wrote the *Concerto for Orchestra* to a commission. It was the first time he had written for a large orchestra for 20 years, since the *Dance Suite* of 1923 in fact. The circumstances were hardly conducive to success. Yet the Concerto proved to be his most popular work, rivalling Stravinsky's *Rite of Spring* and Prokofiev's *Classical Symphony* as the most frequently played orchestral pieces of the century. Although it makes more concessions to public taste than most of his earlier music, it is a brilliant, exuberant work, full of humour and light of touch, with all the hallmarks of Bartók's unique, dynamic style.

The year before it was composed, 1942, Bartók was perhaps at his lowest ebb. Although the doctors could not, or would not, tell him what was wrong, Bartók had begun to experience the early symptoms of the leukemia that eventually to kill him. He suffered a continual fever and his weight dropped below 90 pounds by the end of the year. He was, at the same time, running out of money. On 21 January, 1943, he gave his last public performance,

playing alongside his wife Ditta, with the New York Philharmonic under Fritz Reiner. Worse still, unhappy in his newly-adopted country of the United States, he had written nothing for three years. The future looked grim.

Bartók's friends looked desperately for something to encourage him. Then Fritz Reiner and the violinist Joseph Szigeti suggested to Serge Koussevitsky, the conductor of the Boston Symphony Orchestra, the idea of a commission through the Koussevitsky Foundation. The Foundation had been formed to commemorate the conductor's wife Natalia who had died the previous year.

All at once, things started to look up for Bartók. The medical treatment seemed to be working and his health suddenly improved. While convalescing at Saranac Lake, away from the summer heat of New York city, his fever subsided and he began to gain weight. He seemed to take on a new lease of life and he started working on the commissioned piece with tremendous enthusiasm.

By September, the new concerto was near completion. A few months later, he

The gloomy, atmospheric introduction to the 'Concerto for Orchestra' may have been inspired by the sight and sounds of the dark woodlands around the shores of Lake Saranac (left) in New England, where Bartók was convalescing as he wrote the Concerto in 1943.

Like the bobbing carousels so popular in his native Hungary (left), the witty second movement of Bartók's concerto runs round and round in pairs, as 'pairs of instruments appear consecutively with brilliant passages'.

wrote a piano transcription of the work. When Koussevitsky finally received the work, early in 1944, he was delighted.

Koussevitsky gave the *Concerto for orchestra* its première on December 1 1944. Bartók was well enough to travel to Boston for the performance and was delighted with the warm reception it was given. He proudly wrote to his friend Mrs Creel that Koussevitsky had said it was 'the best work for orchestra in 25 years'. With a touch of irony, Bartók added that this even included the works of the conductor's idol Shostakovich. Sometime later, Koussevitsky asked for an alternative ending. Bartók finished this in spring 1945, a few months

before he died, and the Concerto is now published with both endings.

Programme notes

Bartók wrote an interesting programme note for the first performance of the *Concerto for orchestra,* explaining why he called it a concerto rather than a symphony, even though it is symphonic in length and structure. He says that it is a concerto because of 'its tendency to treat the single instruments or instrument groups in a "concertant" or soloistic manner'. In this way, it shows off the many facets of a well-disciplined modern orchestra.

The Concerto, like so much of Bartók's music, owes a great deal to his passion for the folk music of his native Hungary, as well as his admiration of a fellow Hungarian Franz Liszt (1811-1886) who pioneered the idea of thematic transformation. Bartók's genius enabled him to assimilate the rich textures of tone and rhythm of Hungarian folk music and create his own inimitable works in the same vein. The complex rhythmic pulses of Hungarian dance-steps echo throughout the Concerto. The complex tonalities too find their origins in folk music, not the modern dissonances of Schoenberg. As Bartók said, 'It may sound odd, but I do not hesitate to

18

The brooding Elegy is the emotional core of the whole Concerto. In it, Bartók demonstrates his genius for transforming the primitive harmonies of Hungarian folk music and the sounds of the countryside into music that is intensely modern and uniquely his own. Bartók's interpretive approach to music is echoed in this Expressionist painting by Franz Marc (right). Here, the woodland night, its animals and birds, are clearly recognizable, but the elements have been reshaped and recoloured to express a personal vision.

Franz Marc 'Deer in a Wood I'. Phillips Collection, Washington. Joachim Blauel/Artothek

say that the simpler the melody, the more complex and strange may be the harmonizations and accompaniments that go well with it.' Bartók proves the point in this Concerto.

Introduction: Andante non troppo; allegro vivace

The Concerto opens with an ominous and gloomy passage, dark as night, for cellos and double-basses. It seems to recall the opening of Bartók's *Bluebeard's Castle*.

Example 1

Trembling strings and a tentative call on the flutes reinforce the dark, nocturnal quality of the music, perhaps inspired by woodland noises at Saranac Lake in the Adirondacks where Bartók was convalescing. The opening is repeated, in various forms, on strings, flute and basses over a quiet drum roll and brass enter quietly. While the horn holds a sustained note, three trumpets repeat a melancholy fanfare. The brass fade away, and the intense orchestral passage that follows is like an impassioned cry. Suddenly, the flutes hold a high lone note like a scream and the melody breaks off. Only the accompaniment continues, moving faster and with a louder and louder drum beat pounding out the rhythm.

A new theme begins the *allegro* (quick) section in a new stricter rhythm. Bartók said that this movement was written in a more or less regular sonata form. The first theme of the section is stated energetically on jagged, rising strings, with beats of unequal length. Then a trombone takes over and, accompanied by fluttering flutes, leads the listener to a tranquil melody on oboe with harp and horn accompaniment – an unusual and exotic combination. With a shocking and hurried return of the opening allegro theme, horns, woodwind and strings jostle upwards as the timpani crash. Then the tranquil mood returns with quiet clarinet flute and English horn (cor anglais) passages only to be shattered by the reappearance of the allegro on strings and low woodwind.

The trombone then begins a brilliant, extended section for alternating brass: first trumpets answer the trombones, then horns carry a clever variation on the allegro theme. The insistent strong figure interrupts the ever more complex set of fanfares. A clash of cymbals returns the music with a thump to the quiet woodwinds exchanging their tranquil theme. The mood of calm has scarcely been re-established when the allegro theme returns, building to a sudden and dramatic fanfare for brass. This single movement encapsulates the transition from despondency to optimism which Bartók said was the intention of the concerto as a whole.

Game of Pairs: Allegretto scherzando

The second movement opens emphatically as the side drum establishes a rhythm for the 'game of pairs' to follow. In his programme notes, Bartók describes the game as:

a chain of independent short sections, by wind instruments consecutively introduced in five pairs (bassoons, oboes, clarinets, flutes, and muted trumpets) ... A kind of 'trio' (a short chorale for brass instruments and side-drum) follows after which the five sections are recapitulated in a more elaborate instrumentation.

This is a very precise description of the music, though it hardly captures the wit and beauty of the movement. Each pair of instruments is separated by the *interval* (number of notes) best suited to its individual harmony: bassoons, a sixth apart; oboes, a third; clarinets, a seventh; flutes, a fifth; and trumpets a second – adjacent notes. The chorale trio is played on trumpets, trombones and a tuba, and offers an old-fashioned, but majestic hymn-like tune.

Example 2

The pairs return in more elaborate passages. After the return of the muted trumpets, the side drum returns to close the movement as it opened.

Elegy: Andante non troppo

This is the emotional core of the whole concerto and like the *Game of Pairs* is in a 'less traditional' form. Bartók himself comments:

The structure of the third movement ... is chain-like; three themes appear successively. These constitute the core of the movement, which is enframed by a misty texture of rudimentary motives. Most of the thematic material of this movement derives from the Introduction.

Indeed the basses play an opening section linked closely to the beginning of the concerto, evoking an atmosphere of melancholy and mystery recalling the *Lake of Tears* section of *Bluebeard's Castle*. Decorative flutterings on alternate clarinet and flute calls are echoed by the harp. These rapid sweeping scales are called *glissando* by musicians, from the Italian for 'sliding'.

A high piccolo note sounds like a plaintive bird-call and suddenly the violins return with the passionate orchestral theme of the first movement. Harps and timpani thicken the orchestral mass of this poignant outcry but the music lapses once more into the mysterious night-scene. A section marked *poco agitato, mosso, molto rubato* returns the impassioned orchestral theme again and leads into a long section of muttering woodwind over

The dreamy strings and woodwind chant of the fourth dance of the Suite are reminiscent of the exotic dances of Arabia (below). Bartók's fascination with Arabic sounds stemmed from his research in North Africa.

In the Hungary of old, recruitment to the army (above) was often accompanied by a dance called the 'verbunkos'. A dozen or so hussars, led by their sergeant, would perform a spectacular dance, alternating rapid and slow figures, accompanied by virtuoso renderings of folk tunes by gypsy musicians. The idea was to excite poor men into joining up. The practice died out when the Hapsburg Empire imposed conscription, but the dances survived. Many composers drew inspiration from the dynamic rhythms and brilliant syncopations of the verbunkos, notably Bartók's favourite Franz Liszt. A melancholy verbunkos forms the middle of the first section of Bartók's 'Dance Suite'.

a shimmering, melancholy background. The elegy drifts away into silence after a sad solo on piccolo.

Intermezzo interrotto

Unison strings trill to open this movement, and add a shiver to the laughter that follows. Then an oboe declaims the principal theme over *pizzicato* (plucked) strings. Other woodwind and horns join in the odd syncopation with harps. A majestic theme enters played on strings with soft harp and timpani accompaniment. Viola and cor anglais repeat this trio melody and then return to the livelier first theme via an oboe solo.

The tempo increases and a solo clarinet sounds out a rather trite-sounding theme, a theme used by Shostakovich in his 'Leningrad' symphony. For Shostakovich, the theme represented the Nazis, but Bartók mocks it with tittering laughter on the strings, guffaws in the brass and woodwind, and a 'raspberry' on brass — the ultimate musical insult. A ludicrous development reversing the drunken tune, is crushed with great finality by tuba, gong and cymbals and the beautiful trio returns. Woodwinds make the transition to the jaunty dance tune.

Finale

This movement, again in sonata form, opens brusquely with a fanfare on horns. The strings are given a *perpetuum mobile* (perpetual motion) theme accompanied by a virtuoso drum part becoming faster and louder as other instruments join in, until there is a brief climax. Then the

theme continues even more wildly with explosions on the tuba and woodwinds. Bassoon and flute carry the orchestra into a section marked *tranquillo* (peaceful).

As the woodwinds begin to speed the music up again, a trumpet announces a second jaunty fanfare supported by full orchestra. Once again the hectic pace is halted by a glissando on timpani, and harps are accompanied by clucking hen-like motifs. A drum-beat marks the return of the perpetual motion theme and tension builds quickly to a climax. Suddenly the concerto returns to the earlier melancholy woodwind and gloomy mists of the nocturnal lakeside. A slow crescendo begins as the perpetual motion string figure raises the entire orchestra from the depths. A resurrection is taking place. At the height of the movement, the fanfare reappears.

Bartók, at Koussevitzky's request, wrote his alternative ending to make the resolution a little less abrupt. The work is now published with both alternatives. Both endings confirm Bartók's own short summary of the concerto:

The general mood of the work represents — apart from the jesting second movement — a gradual transition from the sternness of the first movement and the lugubrious death-song of the third, to the life-assertion of the last one.

Dance Suite

20 years separate the *Concerto for Orchestra* and the *Dance Suite* — 20 years in which Bartók wrote chamber music,

notably the string quartets, unrivalled by any composer since Beethoven. Interestingly, the *Dance Suite,* like the concerto was written to commission. Indeed, it was his first commission.

He completed it in April 1923 and it was first performed on November 19, 1923 at a celebratory concert to mark the union of Buda and Pest. Dohnányi and Kodály also had new works performed. The first performance did not go well, mostly, Bartók felt, due to under-rehearsals. But after some alterations, the *Dance Suite* was performed again in Prague in May 1925 with great applause.

Programme notes

Although the suite does not draw on specific folk tunes, it represents much of the research Bartók had done on Hungarian, Rumanian and Arabic sources in earlier years.

I Moderato

The first movement opens with a staggering, vaguely Arabesque theme on bassoons, contrasted with piano and strings.

Its tottering quality is continued on oboe with pizzicato strings. A central lively section for trumpet gives way to a return of the original theme. A violin and harp introduce a sad and beautiful theme reminiscent of the *Verbunkos,* a kind of Hungarian recruiting dance, (usually in two sections), that contrasts effectively with the violent movements surrounding it. A brief woodwind reference to the theme ends the dance.

II Allegro molto

This movement is a dynamic dance accentuated by trombone glissandi, and a trumpet fanfare. The verbunkos theme returns, first on oboe, then on strings, and finally clarinet.

BÉLA BARTÓK

TANZ-SUITE – DANCE SUITE

PARTITUR   FULL SCORE

UNIVERSAL-EDITION

Understanding music: the growth of percussion

Much of 20th-century orchestral music is characterized by the growing dominance of percussion – a once poor relation of the other orchestral sections. Yet prior to the 20th century one of the most curious things about Western 'classical' music was the impoverishment of its percussion. Beethoven, for instance, rarely asked for anything beyond the timpani. And, in general, other percussion instruments were reserved for picturesque effect, as when Mozart uses triangle and drums to add a Turkish flavour.

However, things began to change around 1900. As part of the widespread increase of interest in new sound colours, composers began to include more and more percussion instruments. At first, the intention was still largely picturesque: Richard Strauss and Mahler, for example, both liked to use cowbells to suggest mountain heights, and Mahler's sixth symphony includes a mighty hammer to strike the implacable blows of fate. And with Bartók's keen interest in folk music with its strong, insistent rhythms, it is not surprising that his music abounds in complex and innovative use of percussion.

Gradually, percussion instruments began to be used more for their sounds rather than for what they suggested. And in this development composers' contact with other music, especially oriental music, was crucial. Debussy, for instance, was impressed by the metal percussion instruments he heard in Indonesian music, and he included small cymbals to great effect in his first important orchestral score *L'apres-midi d'un faune.* Then Stravinsky, attempting to evoke an ancient, savage culture in *The Rite of Spring,* made powerful use of drums and cymbals.

Edgard Varèse learned from both these composers and, around 1920, began to include large percussion sections within his orchestra, using all the usual instruments (drums, triangle, wooden blocks, cymbals and so on) as well as others introduced from jazz or from exotic music. Varèse is generally credited with the first western work for percussion alone, his *Ionisation* (1931) for an orchestra of thirteen players; though in fact, this distinction should really go to Stravinsky's ballet, *The Wedding* (1923), where the voices are accompanied by an orchestra of assorted percussion instruments and four pianos, clattering like xylophones.

The xylophone itself, at this time, became an important part of the orchestra, and was used to great effect by Schoenberg among others. The xylophone, like the piano, offered the facility of a percussive sound with a wide range of pitches. Other instruments with this facility include the celesta, introduced by Tchaikovsky in his ballet, *The Nutcracker,* and the vibraphone, which Berg adopted from jazz for his opera *Lulu.* When used in groups, instruments of this kind readily evoke the effects that had so appealed to Debussy, and there are notable evocations of this kind in works by Messiaen, Boulez and Britten.

But this is just one aspect of the percussion revolution. Percussion instruments can also be used to put the emphasis on rhythm, acting merely as 'noise-makers' without producing any distinct pitch. Varèse's *Ionisation,* for example, has no clearly pitched material other than the bell sounds of its ending. Stockhausen, on the other hand, in his work *Zyklus,* took the opposite tack and made a point of making the transition from noise to pitch. Composed in 1959, this was also the first work in the western repertory for solo percussionist, and it requires the player to perform within a circle of numerous instruments: xylophone, vibraphone, drums, gongs and rattles.

Yet another way of using percussion instruments is as a source of creating new pitches outside the scope and conventions of western musical instruments. Composers wanting to work with *microtones* (intervals smaller than semitones), for example, had found it hard to manufacture the microtonal equivalents of highly developed conventional instruments, and hard to train musicians to play microtones accurately. But a microtonal xylophone or metallophone can be constructed quite easily and, once constructed, can be played without any special training. The American composer, Harry Partch (1901–76) built his own instruments along these lines to play music in a new harmonic system of his own.

Other American composers, too, have made a particular point of using home-made percussion instruments. Much of the early music of John Cage (b.1912) was composed for a percussion orchestra he directed, and within which he included not only conventional instruments (even the piano), but also tin cans and electric buzzers. Subsequently, composers have made use of pistols, sirens, spring coils, chains and even wine glasses for percussion effects. Others continue to use the wide range of instruments introduced by Varèse, Xenakis and Stockhausen and also to use the impressive skills of a number of percussion virtuosos who have emerged since World War II.

III Allegro vivace
After the violence of the second Hungarian dance, this one begins cheerfully with a Rumanian rhythmic drive on the oboe and clarinet. The strings join and the orchestral texture thickens. A central section alters the key before the first theme returns embellished by woodwinds, piano and percussion.

IV Molto tranquillo
The dreamy quality of the divided strings and the hypnotic woodwind chant confirms Bartók's judgement that this dance is 'entirely' Arabic.

V Comodo
The fifth dance is in two major sections. As

The text in the image reads: "Vágod a Galgamácsai gyermeksereg"

Great interpreters

Sir Georg Solti (conductor)

In many ways, Sir Georg Solti is the ideal conductor for Bartók. Like Bartók, Solti was born in Hungary, though in Budapest rather than in the country, on 21 October 1912. Like Bartók too, Solti studied music at the Liszt Academy in Budapest. Indeed, at the Academy, he was actually taught by Bartók, as well as Bartók's teacher Dohnányi and his friend and collaborator Kodály. And when the Nazis threatened Hungary in 1939, Solti, like Bartók, left the country of his birth for good.

In 1939, Solti had only recently made his debut as a conductor and found it difficult to get a permit to work as a conductor in his new home, Switzerland. He returned to playing the piano and won the Geneva International Piano Competition in 1942.

After the war, however, he conducted *Fidelio* for the American military in Munich and was made musical director of the Bayerische Staatsoper in the city. His six years with the company were immensely successful and the Bayerische Staatsoper earned him an international reputation. Meanwhile, Solti embarked on a very successful career as a recording artist. Indeed, few conductors have shown such an understanding of the demands and technicalities of this medium. With the producer John Culshaw, Solti was a pioneer of the use of stereo techniques to capture the sheer presence of opera, and their version of the complete *Ring* cycle of Wagner in 1966 was a landmark in the history of operatic recording. Solti has won many awards for his superb recordings.

From the Bayerische Staatsoper, Solti moved in 1952 to an equally successful career in Frankfurt. After a performance of *Der Rosenkavalier* in Covent Garden in 1962, he was appointed musical director there and transformed Covent Garden into one of the best opera houses in the world. Solti took on British nationality and received a knighthood before becoming conductor of the Orchestra de Paris (1971-5) and conducting the *Ring* cycle at the Bayreuth Festival in 1983.

Juli Dudas 'The Children of Galgamasca Dancing' Jean-Loup Charmet

The 'Dance Suite' resounds with the wild and exciting music of the Hungarian folk dances (above) that through his painstaking research Bartók did so much to preserve.

Bartók said in a letter to a friend, 'the theme of no. 5 is so primitive that one can only speak of a primitive-peasant character . . .' The dance begins with a driving rhythm, reinforced by calls on the brass. A new and faster brass theme with percussion reminds us of Stravinsky in the *Rite of Spring*. The rhythm changes again. At the wildest point, the beautiful verbunkos theme returns on strings and harp before the full orchestra propels the piece to a powerful and abrupt conclusion.

FURTHER LISTENING

Piano Concerto No. 3
Written at the very close of his life, this concerto is one of Bartók's warmest and openly beautiful works. It is full of joy and a refreshing love of life and the natural world. Thus it is a completely optimistic piece, with a lucidity of texture and clarity of line which gives the work such a feeling of inner peace.

Piano Sonata
In the 1920s Bartók wrote a series of major solo piano works which he could use on his own concert tours in Europe. Out of this period came the *Piano Sonata*, perhaps the supreme example of his piano writing, and a work in which distinctively folk-like music is made to pour from the most un-folk-like instrument in concert music.

The String Quartets
Bartók composed six string quartets, spanning the period from 1908 to 1939. As a group they stand as one of the great monuments of 20th century music. Each one is, in its own unique way, a masterpiece, and each reflects the stylistic and thematic concerns of the composer at the time of its writing.

BBC Hulton Picture Library

IN THE BACKGROUND
'Wild beasts'

Bartók's 'modern music' was scorned as incoherent and ugly. The same response greeted Modern Art, which broke with old techniques and values in an attempt to express something new.

Henri Matisse (above), leader of the first new movement in 20th-century art – Fauvism.

Edouard Manet's The Luncheon on the Grass *(left) shocked the Parisian art world in the 1863 Salon des Refusés exhibition with its portrayal of a nude woman sitting casually on the grass with clothed men.*

In the short but dynamic period between 1905 and 1925 'Modern Art' was born. And the innovations in European art that came about in this time laid the foundations for nearly all the creative developments which followed over the years, right to this day.

As the 20th century opened the world of art was dominated, as it had been throughout the latter part of the 19th century, by French artists and the influences of Impressionism and Symbolism – movements which were themselves the forerunners of the 'new' art of the 20th century. Then, in 1905, in an attempt to break new ground, the Fauves and Expressionists burst on the scene, followed by the Cubists, the Suprematists and abstract painters, the Dadaists and, finally, the Surrealists.

Not all these movements are clearly defined – artists changed direction and often became part of several different movements. The whole period is one of cross-fertilization and change, but after Fauvism, there was no looking back.

Forerunners of modern art

For about 500 years until the advent of the Impressionists, almost all artists had been striving to portray the world in a representational way – trying to capture on canvas the image of a scene, a face, an object, in the way the eye sees it, as accurately as possible. Then, around the mid-19th century, with the advent of popular photography, the artist's world changed. The camera blinked its automatic eye and, suddenly, the representational artist seemed to be left without a role – there was little point in using paints to record scenes and faces in a straightforward way when the camera could do a better job. What, then, could the artist do that the camera could not? For the Impressionists, the answer lay in trying to capture the fleeting effects of light and atmosphere and analysing the way colours work together. With Post-Impressionist and Symbolist artists however, came a more fundamental step in the development of artistic styles designed to show not only what they saw but also how they *felt* about the world around them. Theirs was a passionate attempt to use paint in an attempt to *express* their own emotional response to what they saw. Van Gogh (1853–90) was perhaps the most significant predecessor of modern art in this respect. He looked constantly to the use of colour to convey his feelings, and in colour he found a means of expression – 'instead of trying to record what I see, I use colour arbitrarily to express my feelings forcibly.'

Gauguin and Cezanne had also experimented

Manet 'The Luncheon on the Grass' 1863. Musée d'Orsay, Paris/Réunion des Musées Nationaux

H. Roger Viollet

Georges Braque (above) at the age of 67. As a young man, he and Picasso worked together 'roped like mountaineers climbing Everest', and became joint founders of Cubism.

intuition and the subconscious when talking about the creative process. Matisse believed that these intuitive feelings were best explored through colour and design. The German Expressionists, however, had strong feelings about the artist's responsibility as a critic of society.

Nolde and Kirchner in Dresden, Kandinsky and Marc in Munich, felt that their paintings should express the problems of modern man, the dangerous materialism of contemporary society. In short, the subject of a picture dictated how it was to be painted, not the other way round.

Kandinsky and his abstract vision

The greatest achievement of the German school, however, was to lay the foundations of abstract art.

along similar lines in the 1880s and 1890s but it was left to the artists of the early 20th century to develop these ideas further.

The Wild Beasts

In 1905 the French art critic Louis Vauxcelles went to view the work of some young painters exhibiting at the Salon d'Automne. Shocked by the violence of the colours in their fiercely painted canvases he labelled the artists 'Les Fauves' – The Wild Beasts – and so baptised the first major artistic movement of the 20th century. The principal Fauvists – Matisse, Derain and Vlaminck, all French – owed much to van Gogh in their approach to their painting. Their paintings were executed in a 'primitive' almost naive way – only the raw form of their subjects was recognizable – and then sometimes barely so – but it was in their use of colour that they sought to express the meanings in their work. And in this they went further than anything their predecessors had attempted. Matisse, leader of the Fauves, stayed longest with the movement and continued painting in this style into the 1920s. Many others, including Vlaminck and Derain began to change course as early as 1908, as other movements modified or stimulated different methods of expression.

In Germany, around the same time as Fauvism sprang up in France, German artists were working concurrently along similar lines. Here, Nolde, Kirchner and Kandinsky became the chief exponents of what was to develop into Expressionism.

Matisse once wrote that he was 'unable to distinguish between the feeling I have for life and my way of expressing it'. Contemporary philosophical thinking already placed increased importance on

No need to distort everyday reality, they concluded, colours and forms are expressive in themselves. The artist who first made this breakthrough was Vassily Kandinsky (1866–1944). Though Russian born and raised, Kandinsky spent most of his working life in Germany. His youth in Russia had given him an intense interest in music, and he was fascinated by the expressiveness of pure colour and pure sound.

It took him some 15 years as a painter to see that abstract art was the best way for him to explore the spiritual world. His first abstract paintings appeared in 1910. His work has been described as 'pure visual music' – a metaphor Kandinsky would have greatly appreciated. For he combined colours and forms in much the same way as a composer orchestrates by setting different instruments against each other.

Cubism

Meanwhile, in Paris, around 1908 there had been an equally revolutionary development: the invention by Picasso and Braque of Cubism. Louis Vauxcelles was again responsible for the name: he said that Braque 'reduced everything . . . to cubes'. Cubism is probably the most complex and misunderstood movement of modern art. Its basic premise was that painting gives an opportunity to study, dismantle and reassemble an object's form and to exploit the infinite scope it offers for invention. Why should an artist restrict himself to one point of view? Why not incorporate what he *remembers* about an object, as well as what he can see of it? Picasso and Braque took still-lifes and figures and used them as starting points for this approach.

The work of Vassily Kandinsky led the way, via Expressionism, to abstract art. His painting Cossacks (left) *is one of a series called* Compositions, *painted between 1910 and 1914, and these mark the transition from Expressionism to abstraction. Here, a castle, five cossacks, their sabres and lances and a flight of birds are all discernible. But the arrangement of shapes and the clash of colours carry the weight of Kandinsky's abstract message.*

Many works were in monochrome, or a very restricted range of colours. This was partly in reaction to the gaudy Fauvists, partly to concentrate attention on structure and form.

Braque employed a 'mobile perspective', moving round his subjects and simultaneously recording different views from different angles, from near-to and far away, with features both remembered and seen. Certain elements are in sharp focus, some are quite blurred – the equivalent, perhaps, of how we recall objects to mind.

Picasso once said, 'I paint my figures as I think them, not as I see them.' The original subject is sometimes very difficult to recognize. Figures melt into the space that surrounds them. The space therefore becomes just as important as the subject.

This relationship between the object and the

space around it fascinated contemporary artists. The next logical step was to do without the object altogether. Thus the Cubists' fascination with form, and Kandinsky's fascination with colour brought them by different routes to abstract art.

In Russia, many collectors bought up the works of Gauguin, the Post-Impressionists, then Matisse and Picasso, almost as soon as the paint was dry. These huge collections had an immense impact on young Russian artists who, between 1910 and 1920, evolved a school of abstract, geometric art in advance of anything in Europe. The most important of these artists was Malevich. He, like the Cubists and Expressionists, felt there was nothing to be gained from studying the visible world, the future lay in finding visual equivalents to conscious and unconscious states of mind.

The style he evolved he entitled Suprematism – shorthand for 'the supremacy of feeling in creative art'. Suprematism was based on the square, which he placed against a white background – the 'white sun of infinity'. So the first Suprematist work was a black square against a white background, though Malevich quickly built up from this an elaborate, highly distinctive vocabulary. Rectangles, squares, circles and lines painted in elementary colours correspond to a whole range of feelings. Squares and rectangles of unequal sizes and shapes, variations of angle and

direction, float against a background to suggest depth. Malevich was hugely influential, both in Russia and, later, in the West.

In wartime Holland, the great proponent of abstract art was Mondrian. Again growing out of Cubism, his was a style more austere than Malevich's, based simply on the square, the rectangle and the right-angle. He used only black and white and the three primary colours, equating these fundamentals of art with the fundamental forces underlying nature. He claimed to seek a purer reality that lay beyond mere superficial appearance. A dynamic tension between lines, shapes and colours animate the canvases. And within his wilfully limited means, he achieved extraordinary variety – just as a jazz musician can create many variations on a theme. (Mondrian was, in fact, an excellent jazz musician.)

Pablo Picasso (far left) was infinitely versatile, contributing to several quite separate schools of art. Co-founder of Cubism and artist of Seated Nude (centre) he pursued Cubism to its ultimate conclusion in abstract expressionism. He did not even confine himself to painting – his pottery is hugely prized.

Dada

Mondrian was appalled by the horrors of World War I. He hoped that his art would help create a better society where such things could not happen. Other artists reacted to the devastation, waste and folly of the war in a different way: with Dada.

Dada was not a person. It was not even a school of art. It was two separate political protest movements – one in New York, one in Zurich – which chose to adopt a child's nonsense word as its name and which violently rejected all established artistic values.

One parent of the rowdy Dada child was the 'Functionalist', Vladimir Tatlin, who argued that fine-art belonged to the capitalist's culture and that artists of conscience should give it up in favour of making chairs and building houses.

The other parent was perhaps the Futurist Movement in Italy, where a new generation of dis-

Composition in Grey, Red, Yellow and Blue *(above) was painted by Piet Mondrian between 1920 and 1926. As early as 1917, he abandoned the landscape painting that had made his reputation, and concentrated on the pursuit of 'pure reality', equating pure colour with the fundamental forces in nature. As time passed, he grew increasingly severe – permitting himself only the use of primary colour blocks.*

The Dada and Futurist movements were scornful of the art establishment and the past, as the quotation splashed across the Dada magazine cover above suggests: 'I don't even want to know if there were any men before me.'

Surrealism took many different forms but its object was always the same – to explore the fantasy world of the imagination and present it as a psychological document. Salvador Dali chose to express himself in an almost photographic style – beautiful, but always slightly grotesque and disturbing – as in The Metamorphosis of Narcissus *(1934) (right).*

Dali's later career was split between painting and making films in the tradition of the 'Theatre of the Absurd'. The still below is from the Surrealist film Le Chien Andalou, *1929.*

contented artists – Boccioni, Balla and Severini – called for museums to be torn down and for artistic taste to stop fawning slavishly on the Old Masters. A work of art was nothing if it was not *relevant.* A work of art was nothing if it did not say anything *original.* Their subjects were often urban and, since cities are full of movement, so were the paintings. Dynamism was all-important. Canvases look like delayed-exposure photography, with a multiplicity of flying limbs. Some subjects are too fragmented by movement to be recognisable. One late convert to Futurism was Marcel Duchamp. When Futurism died in the war, Duchamp's savagery found its outlet in Dadaism.

In New York in 1915, Duchamp and Picabia (both French) were central to the Dada protest movement. They made their protest by ridiculing conventional sensibilities. Man was being depersonalized by the machine: as a protest Duchamp produced his 'ready-

One important name to emerge from Dada was that of Jean (Hans) Arp. He became intrigued to know how the laws of chance affected the creation of a work of art, suspecting that the subconscious mind is heavily involved. His first work, *Collage with squares arranged according to the laws of chance,* was created by tearing up pieces of coloured paper and letting them fall haphazardly on to another sheet of paper, then fixing them where they fell, with additional shapes added as suggested by the initial pattern.

Towards 1918, the two Dada movements met, merged and became closely identified with the revolutionary left-wing politics of the time. But, whereas to sow confusion and dismay in bourgeois minds was an end itself to some Dadaists, others had more positive aims. Arp, for instance, said: 'We were looking for an elemental art that would, we thought, save mankind from the raging madness of those times.'

Cynicism and scorn eventually exhaust themselves when there is nothing left to deride. The shocking ceases to shock. So, in about 1920, Dada died though its ghost has been seen many times since World War 2. The positive offshoot that grew out of it was Surrealism. This movement, too, encompassed more than painting. Its first manifestation was written, its first proponent André Breton, who wrote the *Surrealist Manifesto* in 1924. He defined Surrealism as 'thought's dictation, free from any control by reason'.

Surrealism and Naivety

Shedding the desire to shock and protest, the Surrealists retained an obsession to get to the origins of art, to recover spontaneity and honesty, and purge themselves of superficial sophistication. The art of other cultures, particularly primitive cultures,

mades'. Everyday things like a typewriter, a comb or a urinal were given new and mysterious titles, signed by the artist and thereby made into 'artistic objects'. A snowshovel, for example, was retitled *In Advance of the Broken Arm.*

In Zurich, Dada centred on the Cafe Voltaire, an artistic club-cum-cabaret where, for two years, a demi-monde of literary and musical figures contributed to all kinds of explosively original performances, demonstrations and exhibitions. Dada found outlets in poetry and literary presentation as well as painting and sculpture. Many of the typefaces now used by printers, for example, date back to that era. Design as a whole benefited greatly from Dada's determination to startle and catch the eye. Dada directed a savage wit at contemporary culture. It interested itself in the subconscious, the childish and the irrational. Its art contrasted garishly with austere Cubism.

Whereas many of the radical, experimental artists abandoned perspective as an outmoded convention, Giorgio de Chirico (right), allied to the Italian Futurists and a precursor of Surrealism, used it in the creation of deeply disturbing landscapes peopled by weird figures. Close enough to reality to be recognizable, surreal enough to be unsettling, his paintings are like bad dreams.

H. Roger Viollet

suddenly found an admiring Western audience. African, Indian and Oriental influences crept in. Naive painters, such as Henri Rousseau, who had been quietly ploughing their own furrows, were feted for their childlike spontaneity and richly primitive qualities.

But above all the Surrealists built on the artistic possibilites of the mind's subconscious – of dreams and Freudian impulses – trying to isolate the nature of thought from the cultural clutter of morality, intellect or aesthetics.

Under the movement's title are grouped vastly different styles. There were Orthodox Surrealists, such as Salvador Dali, Rene Magritte and Max Ernst. Their 'hand-painted dreams' pervade the art of the 1920s and 1930s. Equally, such abstract artists as Miró and Paul Klee accounted themselves Surrealists.

Paul Klee exhibited at the first Surrealist exhibition in Paris, 1925. He claimed to be 'possessed by colour', and entrusted his work to the demon 'intuition', refusing to decide on a theme or title until a work was finished. His work is compulsive – but not haphazard: his preoccupation is in placing symbols in a pure formal harmony with one another. In this respect he can be allied to Miró.

Before the dust settles

Almost all the movements that have arisen since can be traced back to the experiments in the first years of the century: black and white Op-Art to Malevich's geometric Suprematism; Warhol's tomato soup cans (countlessly reproduced or vastly enlarged) to Duchamp's 'Urinal'; Henry Moore's semi-abstract sculptures to those first Cubist invitations to examine 'the spaces in between'; Marc Rothko's rectangles of colour to Matisse's blocks of counterbalanced primary paints . . .

The determination to wrest art from the art gallery and the bourgeoisie has taken the form of Environmental Art (canvases too large to be displayed in a gallery) and even Destruction Events in which works of art are themselves obliterated. Ironically, the 'man-in-the-street' has been the first to condemn such *avant-garde* art, the diletante bourgeois the first to invest it with monetary value.

Only with hindsight can the genuine achievements of any movement be appreciated. As Herbert Read has written: an era 'leaves behind it, when the dust has settled, a few genuine works of art'. The dust has only really begun to settle over the first half of the 20th century.

Elements that concerned the artistic innovators of the early 20th century are all reflected in the work of Henry Moore, the British sculptor. His sculptures do not seek beauty, but admire rather the brute forces in Nature and in the human body in particular. He touched briefly on abstract means of expression, but was drawn more towards Surrealism. Like the Cubists, he invites the viewer to observe the spaces between the mass, volume and texture. All of this is contained in the 'Family group', right.

Henry Moore 'Manquette for Family Group' The Tate Gallery, London

THE GREAT COMPOSERS

Igor Stravinsky

1882–1971

Tirelessly productive all his long life, Igor Stravinsky has become the acknowledged giant of 20th century composers. His influence on both his contemporaries and on later generations of composers was overwhelming. He created one masterpiece after another yet never failed to sound fresh and new. He borrowed forms, ideas and styles from the past, but made music that was completely his own. Amongst his very best works stands the surprising and mesmerising Rite of Spring, analysed in the Listener's Guide *with the atmospheric cantata The King of the Stars. The Rite of Spring has been acknowledged as the major transitional work of 20th century orchestral music. The work is a ballet score composed for Sergei Diaghilev's Ballets Russes, studied in* In The Background, *but its power is so remarkable that it is usually played as a concert work.*

Igor Stravinsky was a poor piano student as a child in St. Petersburg, preferring improvisation to routine practice. In 1902, the great Russian composer Rimsky-Korsakov recognized the genius of Stravinsky's experimentation and took him under his wing for private lessons. After Rimsky-Korsakov's death, Stravinsky wrote two remarkable scores for the Ballets Russes, The Firebird and Petrushka; his third commission was for The Rite of Spring, a work that not only made his reputation but revolutionized 20th century orchestral music. He lived in Switzerland and France over the following years, composing a stream of remarkable compositions. He toured all over the world in the 1920s and settled in America in 1939. He remained active as a conductor and in 1962 made a triumphant return to his homeland of Russia, consolidating the full circle of his worldwide acclaim. He died in New York in 1971.

COMPOSER'S LIFE
'I am Russian'

An intellectual, cosmopolitan Russian emigré, Stravinsky rocked the world with his startling, dynamic music, but came to be acknowledged as the greatest 20th-century composer.

Stravinsky remains the great giant of 20th-century music, the man who, more than anyone, assured the break with the romantic traditions of the 19th century and led music forward into the modern world. He lived a Frenchman and died an American, but he was born in Russia and during years of exile he grieved – in life and in his music – for the country of his birth. Likewise he remained true to the Russian Orthodox faith, keeping icons, observing feast days and dedicating his most profoundly religious works to 'the Glory of God' – though, he admitted, 'like those of Haydn, all my works are so dedicated.' Out of Russian Orthodoxy came a lifelong fascination for ritual and order, a fascination which inspired such works as *The Rite of Spring,* and instilled a general respect for convention that meant he could never be 'even the nicest anarchist!'

Physically, Stravinsky was small and slight with disproportionately large hands – craftsman's hands, as he called them – and, despite a rather awkward frame, he was a graceful, charismatic figure. His intellect was sharp but logical and he had a highly organized 'world view'. Not content simply to be well-informed, he craved a specialist's knowledge of every subject and was an avid reader – his Los Angeles library contained 10,000 books! But however weighty the topic, his impish sense of humour was always near the surface and he was a gifted raconteur, especially under the influence of alcohol. (He was extremely partial to wine and whisky; he spurned water as only useful 'for the feet'!!)

He worked tirelessly, sometimes for 18 hours at a stretch, despite being plagued with ill health all his life. Tuberculosis, typhus, bleeding ulcers, hernias, crippling headaches and insomnia all afflicted him at one time or another. The range of pill bottles surrounding his plate at the dinner table once provoked the comment from W. H. Auden that 'the most stable business in the world would be a pharmacy next door to Stravinsky!' But time and again his titanic energy and love of life won through illness, spurring him on into a productive old age.

A Russian childhood
Stravinsky was exposed to music from the day he was born on 17 June 1882. His father, Fyodor Ignatievitch, was a famous opera singer with the Mariinsky Theatre who had impressed Glinka and Rimsky-Korsakov with his performances. His mother,

When this picture was painted in 1915, Igor Stravinsky was only 33, yet he was already internationally acclaimed as one of Europe's brightest and most original composers.

Anna Kyrillovna also sang, and played the piano exquisitely. It was from her, as Stravinsky's memoirs relate, that he 'inherited the valuable ability to read orchestral scores at sight.'

But it was not until he was nine that Stravinsky began to study the piano and music theory and clearly preferred improvising his own pieces rather than struggling with routine practice. These improvizations sowed the seeds of the musical revolution he was to create later.

During his years at the Gurevitch School in St. Petersburg, he made few friends and was, by his own account, a very poor pupil. Invention at the keyboard banished loneliness, as did the yearly summer expeditions to join his cousins on the family country estates at Pechisky and, later, Ustilug where he could enjoy music-making, painting, and the kind of friendship he was never able to find at school.

Nevertheless, his interest in music was far from the consuming passion it was to be later. And in 1901, Stravinsky followed his parents' advice and enrolled in St Petersburg University to study law. Yet it was not long before music began to assume a more important role in his life. His early efforts at improvisation flowered into serious experiments in composition, and criminal law and legal philosophy started slipping into the background of his life. The idea of being a composer took hold firmly. He began to

Stravinsky's parents, Fyodor and Anna (left), provided a rich musical background for the young composer. From his nursery, Igor would hear his father practising for his many operatic roles, and as he grew older he was allowed to explore his father's extensive library of music.

In the summers of 1891 and 1892, the Stravinsky family stayed in the country at Pechisky (bottom left). It was here that Igor met his cousin Katerina, the girl who became his dearest friend and later his wife.

Theodore Stravinsky

wonder whether to enrol in the St Petersburg Conservatoire.

It was at this time that Stravinsky became friendly with a fellow student, Vladimir, the youngest son of the great Russian composer Rimsky-Korsakov. Then in 1902 Stravinsky met Rimsky-Korsakov himself. On hearing Stravinsky play, Rimsky-Korsakov advised Stravinsky not to go to the St Petersburg Conservatoire, where he might become discouraged by the rigid academic approach – 'Instead' wrote Stravinsky later, 'he made me the precious gift of his unforgettable lessons.'

The master-pupil relationship developed into close friendship and Rimsky-Korsakov took on a fatherly role in Stravinsky's life, particularly after the death of Fyodor in 1902. Friendship with Rimsky-Korsakov also gave Stravinsky an entreé to St Petersburg musical life and he began to attend soirées and 'Evenings of Contemporary Music' held to air new works by German and French as well as Russian composers. He was particularly fascinated by the music of Debussy which seemed to inhabit its own unique sound world. But Rimsky-Korsakov warned: 'better not listen to him; one runs the risk of getting accustomed to him and one would end by liking him.'

Triumph and tragedy

In 1905, he graduated successfully in law from the St Petersburg School, but he had no intention of following a legal career. He was now 23 and, as he later wrote, 'at this time, my adolescence came to an end'. He made two important decisions. The first was a total commitment to music. The second was his engagement to his cousin, Katerina Nossenko. Throughout Stravinsky's unhappy school days Katerina's kindness and affection had been a vital support and, over the years they had become very close. They married the following year, and the couple set up home in St Petersburg but during the summer they returned, as they always had, to the family at Ustilug where Stravinsky found he could work in peace. Their first child, Fyodor was born in 1907 and their second, Ludmilla, the following year.

The year 1908 was to hold a sad as well as a happy event for Stravinsky. Early in the summer, he completed an orchestral fantasy called *Fireworks,* to honour the forthcoming wedding of Rimsky-Korsakov's daughter, Nadieshda. Stravinsky posted the completed manuscript to Rimsky-Korsakov from Ustilug, seeking his approval. But the parcel crossed with a telegram from St Petersburg informing Stravinsky of his mentor's death. Shortly afterwards the parcel came back unopened and marked 'Not delivered on account of the death of the addressee'. Stravinsky hurried to join the family for the funeral and later said:

It was one of the unhappiest days of my life. But I was there, and I will remember Rimsky in his coffin as long as memory is. He looked so very beautiful I could not help crying.

Fireworks was later given a public performance in St Petersburg and among those present in the audience was the dazzling impresario Sergei Diaghilev. Diaghilev had, in 1908, successfully staged Russian music and opera in Paris and was now planning to introduce Parisians to Russian ballet. On hearing *Fireworks* Diaghilev immediately became

convinced that Stravinsky was the composer he needed to complete his team.

Stravinsky was quite happy to orchestrate the music for the opening season of Diaghilev's new ballet company in 1909. Then in 1910, Diaghilev found himself without a composer for his ballet on the legend of the Firebird after Anatol Liadov pulled out. It was Stravinsky who came to the rescue and created the score that was to make him the toast of Europe.

The 1910 première of *The Firebird* was greeted ecstatically by the Paris audience. After the final curtain Diaghilev came up to Stravinsky supporting a man on his arm whom he introduced as Claude Debussy. Thus began a friendship which was to last until Debussy's death.

'Petrushka' and 'The Rite of Spring'

The name 'Petrushka' or 'Little Pierrot' came to Stravinsky one day while he was walking along by the sea at Clarens. Typical of his less than solemn approach to musical tradition, he pictured 'a puppet suddenly endowed with life, exasperating the patience of the orchestra with diabolical cascades of arpeggios.'

In Paris, on 13 June 1911, Petrushka, the pierrot who survived murder to jeer and taunt the audience, was premièred with even greater success than the

Stravinsky's cousin Katerina (right) gave him the warm companionship he badly needed throughout his youth. As he explained later, 'I was a deeply lonely child, and I wanted a sister of my own. Catherine . . . came into my life as a kind of long-wanted sister in my tenth year. We were from then until her death extremely close, and closer than lovers sometimes are, for mere lovers may be strangers though they live and love together all their lives.'

Theodore Stravinsky

Some of the world's leading avant garde artists designed sets for Stravinsky's ballets, from Picasso to David Hockney. The sets for the 1928 production of 'Petrushka' by the Krolloper in Berlin were designed by Ewald Duhlberg. Shown left is his sketch for the set for the opening scene in the fairground. Duhlberg's design was innovative in that it broke away from the traditional Russian setting of the story and showed instead a more cosmopolitan world.

Theatermuseum, Köln

Firebird. Debussy's praise was unstinted. 'Dear Friend, thanks to you I have passed an enjoyable Easter Vacation in the company of Petrushka, the terrible Moor and the beautiful ballerina . . . You will go much further than "Petrushka", it is certain, but you may be proud of the achievement of this work.' These were prophetic words, for within two years Stravinsky had created one of the undisputed monuments of 20th century music, his controversial ballet score *The Rite of Spring.*

'And here', as the composer's son has written, 'let us stop a moment and consider. Is not the astounding creative vitality of this young 30-year-old musician a

Stravinsky met Vera de Bosset (right) when she was acting in 'The Sleeping Beauty' in London in 1923. Vera was married to the Russian artist Soudekeine at the time but her relationship with Stravinsky flourished and, 17 years later, she became his second wife.

Roger Viollet

matter for wonder? In three years, 1910–13 he has written the three masterpieces that are to place him at the peak of his reputation – *Firebird*, *Petrushka* and *The Rite of Spring* – and at the same time, like any patriarch, he has made provision for the upkeep of a family living in a perpetual state of nomadism.'

Exile
As it happened, the nomadic state was soon to be terminated by the outbreak of war. Switzerland, which had so far been an occasional temporary refuge, now became home. With the onset of war, commissions from the Ballets Russes dried up, Stravinsky's publishers were out of reach in enemy territory and he could no longer depend on the income from his Russian estate.

'But, throughout the whole period when we were waiting to go back to Russia it was my Russian past which preoccupied me most,' declared Stravinsky, and after his death his son Fyodor reminisced: 'I think he realized in his heart he would never go back to Russia, so his love for his country and his homesickness increased.' A stream of Russia-inspired compositions resulted. He wrote Russian songs and choruses and a number of his best loved works included *The Soldier's Tale* based on a Russian folk tale – a colourful shoestring entertainment for war –

and *Mavra* a comic opera based on a Pushkin story.

Stravinsky was not alone in his grief for Russia. His compatriots from the Ballets Russes shared his exile – Nijinsky, Massine, Fokine, and, of course, Diaghilev, to whom Stravinsky dedicated the work that most expressed his longing for his homeland – *Les Noces* (The Wedding). It was a ballet of peasant custom and religious ritual, born of the same spirit as *The Rite of Spring*. Stravinsky, ever fascinated by the subject of ritual, later recalled sounds of religious rite echoing in his mind as he wrote. And when he played parts of *Les Noces* to Diaghilev on the piano, the great impresario wept, saying it touched him more than

In 1942, the Ringling Brothers circus, with an eye for publicity, commissioned Balanchine and Stravinsky to score a ballet for them. The 'ballerinas' for 'The Circus Polka' were to be elephants! The performances in Madison Square Garden (programme cover right) were, needless to say, a massive success.

anything he had ever heard.

Although his family had now settled down at Morges in Switzerland, Stravinsky himself was always on the move, always possessed by the urge to travel. Though exiled from Russia, he had become a celebrated international artist.

'But after a while', as Stravinsky recalled, 'I became tired of the provincial life in Switzerland. I felt drawn back to the centre of things. Paris!' And in 1920, he moved his family to the French countryside where he was able to work peacefully in between frequent trips to Paris. As ever life involved constant travel, and in 1921, Stravinsky joined the Ballets Russes on tour in Spain and England, where he heard the concert première of *The Rite of Spring*. While in London, Diaghilev planned a revival of *The Sleeping Beauty* at the Alhambra Theatre, and Stravinsky agreed to help with the score. In the cast, playing the non-dancing role of the Queen was Vera de Bosset. Stravinsky was enchanted by the young Russian actress and Vera was captivated by the charismatic composer. Soon they were spending as much time as possible in each other's company. Surprisingly, despite his passion for Vera, he did not neglect his wife and family. And Katerina, devoted as she was, showed saint-like understanding, even to the point of befriending Vera.

On Tour

The 1920s saw Stravinsky travelling continuously all over Europe and as far afield as the USA where he was given a tremendous welcome. This meant that he had little time to devote to the Ballets Russes, and he accepted no more commissions after *Pulcinella* (1920).

But Diaghilev was not happy to lose a grip on his protégé. Nor was he especially mollified by the present of one of Stravinsky's greatest works, the Latin opera-oratorio *Oedipus Rex.* On the contrary, he called it 'a very macabre gift'. Then Stravinsky accepted a commission from Ida Rubinstein to write the ballet *The Fairy's Kiss,* based on music by Tchaikovsky. To Diaghilev, Stravinsky's use of 'classical' material was little short of treason, but there was no opportunity to heal the breach for when, in August 1926, Diaghilev died in Venice, the two men had not spoken for six months. Stravinsky was mortified for, despite many quarrels, they had been close: 'I gave myself up to mourning a friend, a brother, whom I should never see again.'

In June 1934, Stravinsky's naturalization papers came through and he became a French citizen. The following year he published his autobiography *Chronicles of my Life* written in French. But Stravinsky was beginning to realize that it was not in France but the USA that his music was finding most sympathy. In 1935 he toured America, again, to great acclaim, and received an invitation to compose the ballet *Jeu de Cartes* (Cardgame) for the newly-formed American Ballet. Other commissions rolled in from America including the chamber concerto *Dumbarton Oaks* and the *Symphony in C.*

These commissions came at a significant moment. Europe was again poised on the brink of World War, and Stravinsky had been shaken deeply by the deaths through tuberculosis of first his daughter Ludmilla, then his wife Katerina and his mother, within months of each other. As if this were not enough, Stravinsky fell victim to the disease himself. He tried to combat ill-health and his terrible grief by throwing himself into his work. By the time war broke out his health

Ringling Bros/Barnum & Bailey Circus

Roger Viollet

It was Aldous Huxley (left), the English writer, who suggested to Stravinsky that the poet W. H. Auden (below) should write the libretto for 'The Rake's Progress'. Stravinsky was absolutely delighted with the results.

BBC Hulton Picture Library

During his life, Stravinsky met and made friends with many of the world's most famous artists and political figures. The picture above shows Stravinsky and his second wife, Vera, meeting President John Kennedy and his wife Jacqueline at the White House in 1962 at a dinner party given in the composer's honour. Stravinsky later remarked that the President and his wife were 'nice kids!' When Kennedy was assassinated on 22 November, 1963, Stravinsky was deeply upset and wrote a unique intimate tribute. His 'Elegy for JFK' was a small piece for baritone and three clarinets, a setting of four verses in 'haiku' style with words by W. H. Auden.

had improved, and he decided to move to America.

Stravinsky called 1939 'the tragic year of my life', but the end of the year was to usher in the sunniest period of his entire life. He lived in a little bungalow in the Hollywood Hills, gladly relinquishing his nomadic existence to feel, at last, part of a community. Then, in 1940, he married Vera de Bosset, and they began a life of happiness together that was to last until Stravinsky's death.

The Rake's Progress

Stravinsky and his wife took American nationality in 1945. By then he was able to say: 'I feel very well, I feel America is my second country.' The same year he signed an exclusive contract with Boosey and Hawkes, the publishers, which brought to an end a long history of copyright and financial problems. It also meant that Stravinsky could, at last, afford the luxury of working without the constant need for commissions. Stravinsky had long wanted to compose a full-length opera, and now seized the opportunity to devote three years to the project. Moreover, he had a subject. While visiting the Chicago Art Institute he had been delighted by a set of Hogarth engravings depicting the Rake's Progress. The combination of crooks and rogues, love and the devil, seemed to suggest a perfect storyline.

On the advice of his friend, the writer Aldous Huxley, Stravinsky asked the poet W. H. Auden to write the libretto. The collaboration was a success beyond Stravinsky's wildest dreams.

The Venice première of the opera was to take place during the International Festival of Contemporary Music 1951, under the baton of the composer himself. The rehearsals went far from

Unlike many 20th century composers, Stravinsky loved taking the baton at concerts of his own music, and continued to do so until he was an old man. Here he is seen during the 1960s (right).

smoothly but the opera survived its first performance and delighted the Venetian audience.

One summer's day in 1948, a letter arrived from a 23-year-old musician called Robert Craft, asking if he could borrow a score for a Stravinsky concert he wanted to conduct in New York. Stravinsky not only lent the score, but generously offered to conduct parts of the concert himself, and the following spring, Craft met the composer to discuss arrangements. The collaboration was remarkably successful and grew into a close friendship.

The involvement of Robert Craft in his life also meant that he could return to the conducting tours

For the 1975 revival of 'The Rake's Progress' at Glyndebourne, David Hockney echoed Stravinsky's original inspiration for the opera, the paintings of Hogarth, in his design for costumes and set (left).

Stravinsky always yearned to return to the country of his birth, but it was not until 1962, 50 years after he first left, that he set foot in Russia once more – he was welcomed ecstatically (below).

David Hockney 1975

that he had previously enjoyed so much. As old age began to encroach on his strength he was unable to undertake all the work himself, but Craft, who had learnt the interpretation of Stravinsky's music at the composer's side, could prepare an orchestra in advance for Stravinsky's final rehearsal and performance. This way the three companions, Stravinsky, Vera and Craft, travelled extensively.

1962 marked Stravinsky's return to Russia after nearly half a century's absence, to conduct his music in Moscow and Leningrad. He was given a hero's welcome, and, according to his niece, thirty thousand people waited in line for the Leningrad concerts.

He had often made such declarations as, 'the greatest crisis in my life was losing Russia', or 'I speak Russian, I think Russian, and, as you hear in my music, I am Russian'. And, as Robert Craft observed in his Russian diary, 'To be recognized and acclaimed as a Russian in Russia, and to be performed there has meant more to him than anything in the years I have known him.'

By 1967, Stravinsky's health was beginning to fail. That year he made his last recording and conducted his last concert – a performance of the *Pulcinella* suite. When he at last became physically incapable of composing he satisfied his need for music by listening to records, taking pleasure in being able to 'listen to and love the music of other men in a way I could not do when conducting my own.' On 6th April 1971, Stravinsky died at his home in New York. His body was carried across an ocean and a continent, then conveyed across the Venetian lagoon to its final destination, the island of San Michele, where he lies buried in the Russian Orthodox corner, close to his friend Diaghilev.

Camera Press

The Rite of Spring
The King of the Stars

The musical forces unleashed by Stravinsky in The Rite of Spring outraged public opinion in 1913. Today an acknowledged masterpiece, it has not lost its power to disturb and excite.

The idea for a ballet based on prehistoric rites celebrating the arrival of spring first came to Stravinsky early in 1910, while he was completing the orchestration of *The Firebird,* the first ballet that he had written for Sergei Diaghilev's Ballets Russes. At the outset, all the composer had in mind was an image. He saw 'a solemn pagan rite: wise elders seated in a circle watching a young girl dance herself to death'. As yet, this was no more than a fleeting vision — the germ of an idea. But Stravinsky soon shared these musings with his friend Nicolas Roerich, a talented painter, stage designer and student of ancient Slavic rites. He was, Stravinsky thought, just the person to collaborate with him on a scenario. Diaghilev, too, was sounded out on the project and responded with enthusiasm, immediately sensing its balletic potential.

The composition of *Great Sacrifice* (as *The Rite* was provisionally called) proved difficult at first. The task Stravinsky had set himself was that of conveying in musical language the surging forces of nature and the most primitive instincts of man. As a Russian he had experienced the coming of spring as a violent eruption of life after a seemingly interminable, cruel winter, and he could imagine the awe felt by his pagan ancestors at this apparently magical deliverance and their impulse to propitiate the god of spring with a human sacrifice.

Musical ideas equal to such themes do not come easily, and while Stravinsky waited for them to germinate he turned his attention to other projects: another ballet, *Petrushka,* some songs and a short cantata for men's voices entitled *The King of the*

Stars. This harmonically complex work, forms a striking contrast to *The Rite;* its remote, detached mood lies worlds away from the frenzied, elemental character of the work that was to follow.

The Rite of Spring

It was not until the following summer of 1911 that thematic ideas for *The Rite* began to form in Stravinsky's mind. At Ustilug, his summer home in Russia, he began making sketches, breaking off only briefly to visit Roerich, who was at the time staying with the Princess Tenisheva at Talashkino, her estate near Smolensk. Inspired by the princess's priceless collection of Russian ethnic art, Roerich had already sketched the backdrops and designed a number of costumes for *The Rite.* Together he and Stravinsky worked on the scenario.

The composition of the new ballet moved more quickly now. In the autumn Stravinsky and his family moved to Clarens, in Switzerland. There, in a rented house, he worked on the score 'in a tiny room . . . an eight-by-eight (foot) closet, rather, whose only furniture was a small upright piano, which I kept muted, a table, and two chairs'. In these inappropriately spartan surroundings the savage rhythms and

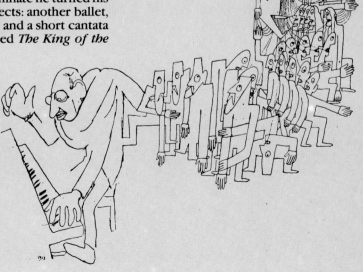

Written as a ballet and based on a story of primitive pagan ritual, The Rite of Spring *evokes an eerie, mysterious atmosphere. The scene (left) was painted from the original stage production.*

Cocteau's drawing (right) of Stravinsky playing The Rite.

electrifying harmonies of *The Rite* took shape. By January 1912 the first half of the score was almost finished.

At the insistence of Diaghilev, the choreography of *The Rite* was entrusted to Vaslav Nijinsky, the great dancer who had created the role of the puppet Petrushka. This did not please Stravinsky, who was alarmed by the dancer's relative inexperience as a choreographer and ignorance of music. He was even more annoyed when – having pushed himself to complete *The Rite* for the Ballets Russes' 1912 Paris season – he was told by Diaghilev that the company could not possibly mount it until 1913, on account of Nijinsky's ill health. Another reason for the delay was that Nijinsky was finding the task difficult – not surprisingly, in view of the music's rhythmic complexity – and was meeting increasing resistance and hostility from the dancers. By way of consolation, Diaghilev invited Stravinsky to accompany the Ballets on its forthcoming European tour. He also promised Stravinsky that the size of the orchestra would be greatly increased in the following season, so making it possible for the music to use larger forces than was originally planned.

Stravinsky took full advantage of this. His orchestration employed a colossal body of players – a larger orchestra than he would ever use again: five of each member of the woodwind family, an outsize brass section comprising eight horns, a piccolo trumpet and four normal ones, three trombones, two tenor and two bass tubas and massive strings to counterbalance this vast array of wind instruments. Only the percussion section is smaller than one might imagine given the predominantly rhythmic nature of the piece.

'Le Massacre du printemps'

The world première of *The Rite of Spring* (or *Le Sacre du printemps,* as it is called in French) took place on 29 May 1913 at the Théâtre des Champs-Elysées, Paris. It was a fiasco without parallel in the history of music. Most of the audience consisted of the affluent, conservative upper and upper-middle classes, who had come expecting pretty music and traditional, virtuoso ballet. But amongst them was a large contingent of artists and students who had been given free standing-room tickets by Diaghilev and who were fiercely determined to applaud anything new and shocking.

The conductor, Pierre Monteux, had scarcely raised his baton for the introduction before murmured protests began issuing from certain parts of the auditorium. Stravinsky's opening bars, for exceptionally high bassoon, clearly augured something disturbing and ominous, and as the music became more strident, the audience became more indignant. When the curtain rose on a

Stravinsky's desire to convey in music the surging forces of nature and the primitive instincts of man comes across in the choreography of Maurice Béjart's 1976 staging of The Rite *(right).*

The awe felt by our ancestors at the apparently magical bursting forth of life in each new spring (below) is the central idea behind The Rite.

group of 'knock-kneed and long-braided Lolitas jumping up and down' (as Stravinsky himself later described them), the storm broke. Whistles and catcalls filled the air. The distorted postures of the dancers inspired one wit to call for 'un docteur!'; another – in response to the girls' leaning their heads on their fists – added 'un dentiste'.

Meanwhile, the *avant-garde* were howling their support and hurling insults at the reactionaries. Fights erupted all over the house – blows were exchanged, clothing torn. In vain, Ravel and Debussy begged the audience to calm down and hear the music out.

Throughout the turmoil the performers carried on valiantly. Monteux 'stood there'

C. Masson. Kipa

Although it is unlikely that the audience would have tolerated Stravinsky's music in any case, their hostility was certainly exacerbated by Nijinsky's choreography. It was soon to be discarded, and was never written down, but by all accounts it was characterized by extremely difficult and awkward movements. Nijinsky understood basically what Stravinsky was evoking in his music, but in seeking to create movements that would express the primitive, barbaric spirit of the work he made the dance unnecessarily complex. 'How far it was from what I had desired,' revealed Stravinsky later. 'In composing the *Sacre* I had imagined the spectacular part of the performance as a series of rhythmic mass movements of the greatest simplicity which would have an instantaneous effect on the audience, with no superfluous details or complications . . .'

The day after the disastrous première, the press took up the conflicts of the previous night with gusto. Most critics roundly condemned the work; 'Le Massacre du printemps' it was dubbed. Stravinsky's revolutionary score was suddenly the most talked-about, the most written-about composition of its time. Considering the musical language to which the public were accustomed in 1913, it is not entirely surprising that *The Rite* caused a furore. One of Stravinsky's biographers, Roman Vlad, has effectively put the matter in perspective:

No one had ever heard music like it before: it seemed to violate all the most hallowed concepts of beauty, harmony, tone and expression. Never had an audience heard music so brutal, savage, aggressive and apparently chaotic; it hit the public like a hurricane, like some uncontrolled primeval force.

After the initial shock, *The Rite* gradually won acceptance by the critics and public. The London première of the ballet a few weeks later was moderately successful. In 1920 Diaghilev re-staged *The Rite* in Paris with choreography by Massine, and this time it was well received. Since then, the ballet has been reinterpreted many times.

(recalled Stravinsky, who was sitting down in front) 'apparently impervious and as nerveless as a crocodile'. But Stravinsky himself was understandably furious. 'I have never been that angry. The music was so familiar to me; I loved it and could not understand why people who had not yet heard it wanted to protest in advance.' Finally, he left the hall, slamming the door behind him.

Backstage he found Nijinsky standing on a chair in the wings, pounding out the rhythm with his fists and screaming directions to the dancers, who, of course, could scarcely hear the music. The choreographer had to be restrained by Stravinsky from dashing on to the stage and making a spectacle of himself.

In violation of the rules of traditional ballet, Nijinsky's choreography for The Rite *required dancers to turn their toes inwards (as shown in this original photograph, right, with Nijinsky himself at the left). It was the ungainly movements of the dancers, as well as the electrifying music, that infuriated the first-night audience and caused a riot.*

Roger Viollet

In the meantime, however, the music of *The Rite of Spring* has found its permanent home in the concert hall and is considered one of the major works of the 20th century. Many more startling sounds now issue from concert platforms, but *The Rite* has lost none of its power. Like all great and complex music, it gives up its secrets slowly, but surely, with each successive hearing.

'I had only my ear to help me,' wrote Stravinsky many years after composing *The Rite*. 'I heard, and wrote what I heard. I am the vessel through which *Le Sacre* passed.'

Programme notes

The Rite falls into two parts each comprising a string of episodes – a vast suite, in effect, of thirteen more-or-less continuous movements linked almost imperceptibly by tiny folk-like fragments of melody and a relentless rhythmic drive. Indeed, it is rhythm, above all, that gives *The Rite* its sense of development, its impetus, its coherence and its constant ability to surprise. On the one hand we are mesmerized by its insistent repetitions and on the other startled by its unpredictability.

Part One: The Adoration of the Earth

This section begins with a remote and primitive chant in the highest register of a lone bassoon:

Example 1

Gradually, other instruments – mainly woodwind – begin to insinuate their way into the picture, and a complex texture is ingeniously woven from their independent melodic strands. The florid mobility of the woodwind writing, the abundance of trills and arpeggios suggest sap rising through plants and the bursting energy of renewing life. For a moment the bassoon is left alone again – suspended, as it were, in a kind of uneasy limbo. But it is only for a moment. Pizzicato violins now herald the arrival of man on the scene in 'The Harbingers of Spring', or 'Dances of the Adolescents', and Stravinsky unleashes savage stamping chords from the full string complement with heavily accented barks from his eight horns to mark out the syncopations.

Example 2

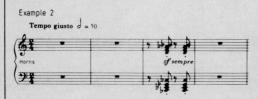

For a few split seconds we are stopped short in our tracks by a forbidding growl from two bass tubas and a fierce outburst from the timpani. The hiatus over, two piccolo flutes and the high piccolo trumpet are quick to set the rhythm in motion again. A heady climax ensues but is soon arrested, as tense *tremolandi* in the strings and three thuds on the bass drum signal the 'Ritual of Abduction'. Stravinsky propels his orchestra into a headlong *presto* here with timpani centre-stage and wild hunting calls from the first two horns.

The brutality is suddenly cut short, though, by quietly trilling flutes, which create a haunting moment of stasis, the first of several to conjure up images of possession, of mysterious ritualistic trances. Heaving basses now drag themselves into a slow, solemn procession, with horns and then flutes leading the cortège ('Spring Rounds'). The climax is monumental: great crashes on the tam-tam (large gong), and trombone *glissandi* like the roar of prehistoric beasts.

A fleeting *vivo* passage takes us quickly into another brief moment of stasis before trombones, tuba and timpani introduce the 'Ritual of the Rival Tribes'. Theirs is a vividly energetic, percussive theme answered by a sort of fanfare motif in the horns. The underlying rhythm soon grows more distinct, rapidly gathering strength and adopting a machine-like regularity. Within a few bars, four tubas are bellowing forth an imposing counterpoint and the clamorous 'Procession of the Sage' begins.

Listen here for the high piccolo trumpet screaming out repeatedly above the fray. Deafening is the onslaught at this point and chilling the uneasy silence that follows in its wake. 'The Sage' rises slowly, his omnipresence depicted in a mere four bars

of music, the last an eerie pianissimo chord on solo strings. Now comes the frenetic 'Dance of the Earth' – a wild eruption of sound in which the very ground we stand on is seemingly torn asunder by a series of seismic convulsions from rapid-fire bass drum, timpani and angry basses. The music becomes ever more frenzied, then, stops abruptly.

Part Two: The Sacrifice
The second section begins with an introduction of chilling bleakness that suggests some extra-terrestrial landscape. The arctic sonorities of the divided strings and echoing horns introduce a serene but weird motif which is taken up again in the 'Mystical Circles of the Adolescents' – this time on violas in six-part harmony. Another idea, introduced initially on alto flute, expands the lyrical dimension of the music still further, but the mood is unmistakably restless and filled with foreboding. The trance-like repetition of a

Roger Viollet

Boccioni 'Stati d'Animo I' Gli Addii, Gallery of Modern Art, Milan

Written for and first performed by The Ballets Russes, The Rite was choreographed by Nijinsky. The notes (left) show some of the original dance movements from 'The Sacrificial Dance' – the only solo in the ballet – related to the music.

In a series of orgiastic bursts of rhythmic fury The Rite ends with the sacrifice (centre) of a girl to the gods to ensure the return of spring.

seven-note theme by strings and muted brass revolves over a monotonous 'tick-tock' pizzicato figure, suggesting a passive submission to a powerful will. This extended moment of uneasy calm eventually erupts into the first of the three dances which will carry the work to its delirious climax. Eleven savage crotchets hammered home by the two timpanists and bass drum player usher in the 'Glorification of the Chosen One' – a brittle, vigorous section marked by brilliant flashes of light from the flutes and piccolo and gusty whoops from the horns. A momentary silence precedes the 'Evocation of the Ancestors', which is built entirely upon a two-note chorale idea in the wind, punctuated by timpani flourishes plunging to sustained pedal-bass notes.

'Ritual Action of the Ancestors', which follows next, is sinister and cat-like – the English horn (cor anglais) and alto flute twisting and turning above hypnotically simple percussion accompaniment. The principal theme here – an unashamedly brazen march-like idea – is given first to muted trumpets and then to the horns, from which it twice roars out triple-forte.

Example 3

Horns (with bells in the air) sounding a fifth lower

The final and longest section of the work is the 'Sacrificial Dance', in which the chosen virgin must dance until she dies of exhaustion if spring is to return. Here the music reaches the peak of its rhythmic fury in a series of orgiastic climaxes. The constantly changing metre and the savage goading of brass and drums vividly evoke the frenzy of the victim. The final moments are stunningly graphic: bass drum and brass have seemingly snapped their last, and the flutes, with a frail upward spiral suggest the maiden's last intake of breath. One final gasp and she crumples to the ground. *The Rite* is accomplished.

The King of the Stars

Stravinsky's miniature cantata for men's voices, *The King of the Stars,* was one of the works which occupied him while waiting for the musical inspiration of *The Rite* to materialize. His text – a visionary poem by Konstantin Balmont, brimful of

Understanding music: 20th-century orchestral music

From the Renaissance onwards European music has been governed by regular patterns in its construction – patterns of melody and harmonic progression, and the ordered, logical development of themes based on the major and minor key system. But the orchestral music of the 20th century marks a break with this past. Consequently, it sounds quite different to the music of preceding centuries and needs to be listened to in a different way.

It was Stravinsky's *Rite of Spring* that marked the turning point and since then hardly any orchestral music of the 20th century has been unaffected by the revolution it caused.

In 'The Rite' Stravinsky invited the listener to focus on the particular qualities of the overall sound and to pay attention to the rhythms within it, or, simply, to be amazed at the effects of the music. He did this by going outside previously held values of musicality in his writing and by using the orchestra in a different way.

In the first place, Stravinsky suddenly presented western music with a new way of considering rhythm. In 'The Rite', there is a return to a more primitive kind of rhythm – the music thumps in emphatic pulsation and flies in a quite unpredictable fashion.

Because Stravinsky wanted great orchestral attack, for effect, he dominated his orchestra not by the strings, as had always been usual, but by the brass, woodwind and percussion. A few years later, in works like his piano concerto and the ballet *Les Noces,* he even abandoned strings altogether – the concerto is accompanied by a wind orchestra and *Les Noces* is for an orchestra of pianos and percussion instruments. With this move Stravinsky ended the strings' traditional leadership of the orchestra and his new stressing of the wind and percussion eventually became characteristic of a great deal of 20th-century orchestral music.

Also, Stravinsky's powerful focus on individual rhythmic pulses led to a relaxation of what had always given western music its flow and continuity – the harmony of the major and minor scales. Here, the influence of folk music was crucial. Like many composers of his time – Bartók was another – Stravinsky had found an alternative to major-minor harmony in the folk music of Eastern Europe. This was often based on very ancient modes (scales). Debussy had earlier shown the way, with his use of the modes that had been preserved in plainsong, as well as others of his own devising (chiefly the whole-tone scale). But Debussy never broke with the major-minor system as decisively as did Stravinsky and Bartók.

At the same time, other composers were looking for further alternatives. Instead of creating different scales, they did away with the idea of scales altogether and freely used all twelve notes in an octave on the keyboard. The so-called 'Second Viennese School' of Schoenberg and his pupils (Berg and Webern) became leaders of this development in Europe while Ives explored similar paths in the United States. In both cases, the effect was a further revolution in the sound of 20th-century music, since to do without the major and minor scales is to do without *consonance* and *concord* (notes which when used together produce a chord which sounds complete in itself, and does not need resolving by another chord). And this had been the very basis of orchestral music. The result of this new approach produced sounds both strange and bewildering, or beautiful and mysterious. Whatever the effect, though, the outcome was to challenge the deepest conceptions of what music ought to be.

Once *The Rite of Spring* had broken the sound barrier in terms of rhythm, orchestration and harmony, composers were quick to take advantage. Schoenberg's breakthrough in atonality had come a little earlier, in 1908, but it was Stravinsky's work that was widely and most swiftly influential. Even Debussy was impressed, as his last works show, and among younger composers, Bartók and Varèse were marked for life by Stravinsky's insistent energy and approach.

Varèse, who emigrated from Europe to the United States during World War I, pursued like no one else the drive towards new kinds of sound. He was one of the first composers to see the potential in electronic music, but he also worked a great deal with percussion instruments, as have later composers such as Messiaen, Boulez and Xenakis.

All this, then, has led to a quite unprecedented diversity of music this century, since no new order has been introduced to replace the old. This is not to say that there have not been attempts at finding such an order: Schoenberg's Serialism and Stravinsky's Neoclassicism are examples. But these attempts have always been equivocal and controversial. Furthermore, there appear to be many more paths that composers have yet to explore. The very essence of 20th-century orchestral music, therefore, is, and remains, one of unbridled adventure.

Tarot card designed by Freda Harris for Alistair Crowley, Warburg Institute. Photo Michael Holford

apocalyptic imagery and symbolism – was, Stravinsky admitted, somewhat obscure both as poetry and as mysticism, but 'its words were good . . .'

Unlike *The Rite, The King of the Stars* had to wait for over a quarter of a century before being heard at all. Some critics have suggested that this strangely elusive opus was no more than a passing gesture, to be disregarded in the final reckoning. But every one of Stravinsky's works marked a development of his creative talent and, as such, all fit together like a jigsaw to form a complete picture of his music.

'The Hierophant'
(left), one of the
characters in the
Tarot deck, is a
majestic figure
similar to that
evoked in the poem
'The King of the
Stars', on which
Stravinsky's
cantata is based.

Stravinsky
dedicated 'The
King of the Stars' to
his friend Debussy
(shown with
Stravinsky in the
photograph
below). Debussy
called it 'probably
Plato's "harmony
of the eternal
spheres"....'

Great interpreters

Michael Tilson
Thomas (left) has
established
himself as one of
the most gifted
American
conductors, and is
noted particularly
for his
interpretations of
twentieth century
music.

Photo Allan Dean Walker. Courtesy CBS Records

BBC Hulton Picture Library

Programme notes

The cantata is very much an atmosphere piece — transcendental, mystical. A big orchestra, similar to that of *The Rite,* is used sparingly: a subtle combination of gently palpitating woodwinds, muted horns and shimmering, multi-divided strings. Nearly the whole of the text is set to chords in four-part harmony. The pace is, for the most part, a slow six beats to a bar; the duration, a mere six minutes. There are no metric surprises, the effect being one of trance-like calm.

Michael Tilson Thomas (conductor)
Thomas was born in Hollywood in 1944. He showed musical inclinations at a very young age, playing the piano by ear when he was five.

By the time he was 20 he was conducting Monday evening concerts at the Los Angeles Museum. He assisted Pierre Boulez at the Ojai Festival in California, then left the United States in 1966 to study at Bayreuth in Friedland Wagner's classes.

In 1968 Thomas was a conducting fellow at Tanglewood, Massachusetts, with the Boston Symphony Orchestra, and was awarded the Koussevitzky Prize, an award in memory of the first wife of one of the Boston Symphony's finest conductors, Serge Koussevitzky. That same year he was engaged as the orchestra's assistant conductor, and in the following year appeared with it as a substitute for the ailing William Steinberg. He was immediately hailed as a brilliant new talent. In 1970 he was appointed associate conductor and then offered the position of permanent conductor. He turned this down to become musical director of the Buffalo Philharmonic. Subsequently he has appeared all round the world as guest conductor, and between 1971-9 he was made principal guest conductor, along with Colin Davis, of the Boston Symphony.

A very adventurous musical spirit, he has a wide repertoire, ranging from music of the Renaissance to electronic music. He has a clear preference for the modern repertoire and among his favourite composers are Ravel, Debussy and Stravinsky.

FURTHER LISTENING

The Firebird
With this ballet Stravinsky made his initial impact on the world of classical music when it was premièred in Paris by Diaghilev's Ballets Russes. It is a colourful, consciously exotic and romantic work with echoes of many Russian forebears, including Rimsky-Korsakov. But the individualism of the young Stravinsky still shows through in the beauty and balance of the orchestral writing. In the concert hall *Firebird* is normally performed in Stravinsky's own shortened concert suite, but the complete ballet is well worth a listen.

Symphony of Psalms
Stravinsky never wrote a conventional symphony; however three of his orchestral works, including this one, are so entitled. This work, a setting of three of the psalms of David, is a symphony in the old sense of the word: that of an orchestral piece of intricate design, here with the addition of voices in a major role. The result is one of the most attractive works of Stravinsky's middle years. It reflects a multitude of intense religious emotions and culminates in an incandescent 'Hymn of Praise'.

Ebony Concerto
No one would claim this as one of Stravinsky's greatest works, but it is an immensely enjoyable one and points up the characteristic breadth of style in his writing. That he could successfully attempt such a pastiche of jazz orchestral writing is remarkable enough, but that he should imbue it with such life and wit is surely quite an achievement.

IN THE BACKGROUND

'Astonish me'

**Sergei Diaghilev, 'the collector of geniuses',
gathered around him dancers, artists and
composers, and created a company that astounded
the world of art – the Ballets Russes.**

'It is my firm belief that human society is divided into three distinct castes: Russian dancers, dancers, and very ordinary people.' With these words Arnold Haskell opened his book *Balletomania* in 1934 – and he was not alone in his opinion. The Russian dancers he referred to were the dancers of the Ballets Russes who reigned over the world of ballet so supremely that, for hundreds of thousands of Europeans and Americans, they stood as giants even in a time of artistic 'greats'. Yet they owed their elevated position to much more than their own dancing abilities. In fact, they owed much to the brilliant overall staging of the ballet productions in which they danced – the productions of the Ballets Russes Company. And behind this great and revolutionary dance company was one man: the creator, organiser and director of it – Sergei Diaghilev.

For the 20 years between Diaghilev's first

Sergei Diaghilev (left) called himself a charlatan and a charmer, with no real talent, but he found his true vocation as an impresario. His first achievement was to open Russian minds to Western art with The World of Art *magazine (below right)., His next was to expose the West to a generation of exceptional Russian artists. 'Remember, remember the ugliness, the triteness, the mediocrity at the beginning of the century,' wrote Emile Henriot in praise of the changes Diaghilev wrought on traditional ballet (below).*

presentation of the Ballets Russes, in 1909, until his premature death in 1929, Diaghilev set the world of art aflame. His vision was to bring together a huge assembly of talent from all the fields of art and unite them to present a balanced, rounded world of illusion and entertainment. This he did with unparalleled success in his Ballets Russes Company.

After Diaghilev's death the spirit of the Ballets Russes lived on in the form of other Ballets Russes Companies, but it was his original idea that was to revolutionize the world of art and dance.

'The World of Art'

Long before Diaghilev set up the Ballets Russes he had showed his individual ideas and his flair for organization. In his home city of St Petersburg, Diaghilev and his circle of friends founded, in 1899, a magazine called *The World of Art* (in Russian, Mir Iskusstra). This gives early clues to his ideas and to his unique sense of artistic presentation. The purpose behind the magazine was to fight Russian prejudice against Western art as, at the time, all art within Russia was dominated by a policy of 'Russian themes for Russian Art'. A notable example of this was classical Russian ballet. This had been the focus of the world as far as ballet was concerned yet it seemed to Diaghilev too claustrophobic – Russian ballet dancers, Russian themes and Russian music. Diaghilev set out to change this nationalist policy by championing 'art for art's sake' and introducing Russia to 'Western' art. In turn he introduced the West to the best of Russian art. He also organized a series of exhibitions in St Petersburg (now Leningrad) which featured Western paintings. And due to the theatrical flair with which he presented them they enjoyed considerable success.

Other exhibitions, even those with exclusively Russian themes, were also a revelation to those who saw them. These reached a climax in 1905 with his exhibition of historical Russian portraits. But in the same year, *The World of Art* ran out of funds and closed. Diaghilev thus turned his attentions abroad. He looked to Paris in particular to forward his ideas,

and took a major exhibition of Russian painting there in 1906, a series of concerts of Russian music in 1907 and a season of Russian opera in 1908. All these became, in turn, the talk of Paris.

Back in St Petersburg at the subsidized Mariinsky Theatre, under the patronage of Duke Vladimir, Diaghilev set to work on the repertoire for a new season of opera and ballet that would be presented in Paris in 1909. Working in committee with his associates Fokine the choreographer, Benois the set

Bakst's superb and exotic programme for the 1911 Ballets Russes season in Monte Carlo (below) shows the kind of design detail which was so typical of the Ballets Russes.

designer and Leon Bakst the costume designer, they began to gather ideas. The repertoire included the ballets *Les Sylphides, Le Pavillon d'Armide* and *Cleopatre,* and the operas *Ivan the Terrible, Prince Igor, Russlan and Ludmilla, Judith* and *Boris Godunov.* Then, just as the repertoire was finalized Duke Vladimir died and the subsidy was withdrawn. All appeared lost until Diaghilev saved the day by calling on financial help from his friends in Paris. This, however, changed the whole situation vis-a-vis Diaghilev's position and his influence on the repertoire. Consequently, the opera was cut to the bare minimum and the ballet emphasized – with Diaghilev changing pieces and introducing others to reflect what he thought the Paris public wanted, as Paris, rather than Russia, seemed to point to the way foward for the company.

Gathering the very best artists and dancers from around him, Diaghilev and his company set off for the 1909 season in Paris.

The Ballets Russes opens

The opening night of the *Ballets Russes* in the Thèâtre Chatelet, which Diaghilev had had specially redecorated and refurbished, was a sensation. A few Russian dancers had been seen, and admired, before in the West. But the impact of a united company, harnessing unmatched artistic talents, staggered the Parisian audience. No Western artists had ever worked together with such commitment and intensity. These ballets were not mere vehicles for virtuoso dancing solos, they were overall images, presented as a unified whole. Maurice Brillant wrote of that first dazzling season: 'All artists understood that this was more than exotic entertainment.'

In due course, Petrushka was danced by Nijinsky to Stravinsky's music and Fokine's choreography, with Benois' designs. In *The Three-Cornered Hat,* Leonide Massine and Tamara Karsavina danced to Massine's choreography and the music of Spain's great composer Manuel de Falla, within vivid yellow sets designed by Pablo Picasso. *The Firebird, The Rite of Spring, Les Noces, Les Biches* and *Apollo* followed, and all were hugely successful.

Even when Diaghilev failed, he failed magnificently. Jean Cocteau, Satie and Picasso combined forces to attempt a 'union of painting and the dance' entitled *Parade.* It scandalized its audiences, But then, to an

The American dancer Isadora Duncan (below) visited Russia early in the 1900s and rocked artistic society. She had no technique, no morals, she lacked sex appeal, and her prancing verged on the ridiculous. But her stage dress and use of non-ballet music had a dramatic and influential impact.

Vaslav Nijinsky and Anna Pavlova in Le Pavillon d'Armide *(right), selected for the first Ballets Russes season. Pavlova finally left the company when she felt it was stifling her stardom. Nijinsky, however, stayed on to become both dancer and choreographer.*

extent, the public relied on Diaghilev to shock them. They could forgive almost anything but conservatism. The man himself tired of the English who were doggedly complimentary about everything he did. But he tired, too, of the Parisians who wanted some new outrage to capture their attention every season.

Nijinsky – 'an angel, a genius'

Though the Ballets Russes did not rely for popularity on the cult of the star dancer, it must owe much of its glory to the quite exceptional talent available at the time of its creation. Destined to become the most famous male dancer of all time, Vaslav Nijinsky was among the artists who travelled to Paris for that first triumphant season. With him was Tamara Karsavina – 'the most exquisite daughter of classical choreography'. She stayed with Diaghilev through thick and thin: through financial instability, internal rifts, and ice ages of critical opinion.

Nijinsky – immensely energetic, unambiguously masculine, and with the on-stage illusion of good looks – was able to fulfill Diaghilev's ambition to put the lead male dancer back on par with the prima ballerina of classical ballet. Women had tiptoed their way towards monopolizing the Western ballet. Now Nijinsky leapt to the centre of the stage and captured the posters, the programmes, and the admiration of his astonished audience.

He captured Diaghilev, too, who needed the

Stravinsky shelved The Rite of Spring *to write* Petrushka *in time for the 1911 season. The design of costumes and scenery (above) was entrusted to Benois, and the ballet was hailed as a sublime unification of dance and painting. Fokine (seen left in* The Firebird *with Karsavina) was both dancer and choreographer in* Petrushka.

companionship and potential of a golden protegé more than he needed an alliance with a woman. He encouraged Nijinsky's secondary career as a Ballets Russes choreographer, and showed great personal kindness to a young man who cut quite a helpless figure off stage. Tragically, Diaghilev's possessiveness soured the golden partnership even before its dreadful end in 1929 when Nijinsky suffered total mental collapse.

New dances to old music

The first choreographer whom Diaghilev used for his Ballets Russes was Mikhail Fokine (1880–1942). This determined and passionate young choreographer did his first work with dance students at the school attached to the great Mariinsky Theatre in St Petersburg. For in choreographing works set in ancient Greece, such as *Acis and Galatea* or *Daphnis and Chloe,* Fokine insisted on abandoning

The artist Jean Cocteau made dozens of lightning sketches (like that showing Stravinsky, Diaghilev, himself and Satie, left) capturing the creative ferment surrounding Diaghilev.

The fly-poster below demonstrates what an ambitious and varied repertoire the **Ballets Russes** *undertook.*

conventional ballet tutus and pointework in favour of presenting a convincingly 'Greek' image. He wanted his student dancers to dance barefoot, though at the Mariinsky was thwarted in this by the strictly observed niceties of ballet convention. However, this radical approach was pre-empted by the revolutionary American dancer Isadora Duncan. In 1904 she had outraged and amazed St Petersburg with her dancing. Grand yet simple, it was set to great classical music by Chopin, Schubert and Beethoven. She performed in bare feet and in a light, flowing, short Greek dress. The idea of dancing to music that had not been intended for the dance inspired others. In 1905 Fokine had set *The Dying Swan,* for the ballerina Anna Pavlova, to music from Saint-Saëns' *Carnival of the Animals.* Then, perhaps inspired by Duncan, he made an entire ballet to orchestrated works by Chopin, revising it in 1909. A Romantic poet dances by moonlight with a winged sylph. In Russia, this version is still danced under the title *Chopiniana.* Later, in 1909, Diaghilev capitalized on the idea and took a modified version of it to Paris. For the Ballets Russes repertoire he

Pablo Picasso's painted set design for the ballet Pulcinella *(below) was used to promote the performance. It appeared on posters and on the programme cover beneath the bold words* Serge Diaghilev. *By 1923 Diaghilev's reputation was such that his name featured prominently, whereas in the early days he kept it out of sight.*

Ballets Russes *became synonymous with the lavish and the shocking. It has been suggested the company contributed to the decadence of the 1920s, but it may have simply reflected the taste of* avant garde *society and the artistic world, for exotic sensuality. At the same time as he was designing the orgiastic* **Scheherazade,** *Leon Bakst painted* **The Pink Sultana** *(left).*

Motley Books

commissioned new designs and gave it a new title to emphasize its Romanticism – *Les Sylphides.* Today it remains one of the most widely performed around the world of all ballets.

Fokine's *Scheherazade* of 1910 for the Ballets Russes was set to a work by Rimsky-Korsakov, and one familiar to concert-hall audiences. He omitted one movement, and though his story was taken from the world of the *Thousand and one Nights,* it used none of the specific tales which had inspired Rimsky-Korsakov's music. Instead, Fokine responded to the structure and the lavish colour of Rimsky's score. The harem setting was designed by Bakst in colours that had never been combined before – great expanses of emerald green against stretches of purple and orange, with cushions and hanging drapes. On the opening night the audience burst into spontaneous applause at their first glimpse of it. Indeed, the production inspired a new vogue in fashionable eastern interior decorations throughout Western Europe before World War 1. Its central performances by Ida Rubinstein as the glamorous and imperious Zobeide, and by Nijinsky as the Golden Slave, became legends of the theatre. Nijinsky, his skin daubed blue-black, stunned the audiences with giant bounds that covered over half the stage.

New music

Of the sixty-eight ballets that Diaghilev presented in 21 years, many were made to existing scores from the concert-hall, or to existing ballet music. The first 1909 season featured no ballet scores written specially for the Ballets Russes. But Sergei Diaghilev, a man of immense foresight and daring, could see the way ahead. He began to commission new scores, looking more and more, with the passage of time, to Western artists and composers. Ravel, Debussy, Richard Strauss, Satie, de Falla, Poulenc, Georges Auric, Daniel Milhaud, Constant Lambert, Henri Sauguet, Lord Berners and Vittorio Rieti all provided scores for new Diaghilev ballets. As for Russian composers – Serge Prokofiev was to provide scores for three ballets, including the last new work Diaghilev would present – *The Prodigal Son.* But by far the most important composer to Diaghilev, and to this century's music, was Igor Stravinsky.

Ida Rubinstein (below) was a pupil of Fokine's and the only non-Russian dancer to go to Paris with the first Ballets Russes. She later studied under Sarah Bernhardt to become an actress (seen here in Secrets of the Sphinx). *Later still, she began a rival ballet company, purloining (as Diaghilev saw it) his artists.*

Stravinsky and Diaghilev – a two-way debt

Stravinsky was involved in the Ballets Russes almost from the start. He was one of several composers whom Diaghilev asked to reorchestrate Chopin's music for *Les Sylphides* in 1909. He was also the first to compose a new score for Diaghilev – *The Firebird* — in 1910. And he worked with Diaghilev right through to 1929.

Diaghilev's audacious taste made the Ballets Russes an ideal vehicle for Stravinsky's rapidly changing musical style. In fact, his next major work for Diaghilev, presented in 1913, was *The Rite of Spring*. The first night was marked by the most violent scenes in the stormy history of Parisian

The Firebird (set design right) was the Ballet's *first wholly original creation, with music, design and choreography all specially commissioned for it. It was an immediate and lasting triumph, made Stravinsky's name, and proved Diaghilev's theatricality, vision and daring.*

In 1929, in an attempt to spark some memory in the vacant mind of Nijinsky after his mental breakdown, Diaghilev brought him on to the stage of the Paris Opera House at the curtain call of Petrushka (below). *Tragically, Nijinsky remembered nothing. From the left: Benois, Karsavina, Diaghilev, Nijinsky, Serge Lifar.*

theatre. Acid critics lambasted it. But Stravinsky wrote that after that tempestuous première Diaghilev took him and Nijinsky to dinner and remarked, 'Just what I wanted.'

The New Classicism

Before the Great War, the Ballets Russes were stylized representations of specific subjects. Several of these subjects were themselves Russian – *Firebird, Petrushka, Rite of Spring,* and the *Polovtsian Dances* from *Prince Igor.* The combination of Russian subjects and Russian artists had a vigour and exoticism that conquered the West. But slowly a new attitude emerged. Subjects became less important, style more so. Diaghilev asked several of his collaborators to revise old music as part of this 'neo-classical movement'. Tommasini worked on Scarlatti themes, Respighi worked on Rossini tunes, and in 1920 Stravinsky worked on Pergolesi music to make *Pulcinella:* old fabric, new styles.

Diaghilev was not solely concerned with novelty. To the great surprise of many admirers, he organized in 1921 a major revival of the great Tchaikovsky-Petipa ballet, *The Sleeping Beauty,* staging it in London at the Alhambra Theatre under the title *The Sleeping Princess.* There were lavish new decor and costumes by Bakst, some revised choreography by

(Above) Nijinsky at the height of his glory, in the role of Golden Slave in Scheherazade. *Over the years his dressers made considerable sums from selling fragments of his costumes.*

Serge Lifar (below) was Diaghilev's last protegé. He later became a central figure in the Ballets Russe de Monte Carlo – *a company set up to continue the spirit of* The Ballets Russes. *He was with Diaghilev when he died, twice restoring his heartbeat when it faltered.*

Bronislav Nijinska, and the Tchaikovsky music was subtly rescored by Stravinsky.

Not restricting himself to ballets, Diaghilev mounted (though rather grudgingly) the première of Stravinsky's opera *Oedipus Rex* in 1927. But he could not always afford to commission new works from Stravinsky, who occasionally provided compositions for organizations other than the Ballets Russes. Tremendously jealous and possessive, Diaghilev bitterly resented the fact that Stravinsky (like Ravel, Massine and Nijinska) did work for the Ida Rubinstein ballet company. He was also annoyed,

to find that in 1928, Stravinsky was making a ballet score for a première in Washington, DC. Stravinsky appeased him by offering the European première of the work to the Ballets Russes. The ballet was *Apollon Musagete,* also known as *Apollo, Leader of the Muses,* or just *Apollo.*

The score was given to Diaghilev's latest choreographer, George Balanchine. Twenty-four years old and musically trained, Balanchine would later say of the music that it changed his life.

Stars and a star-maker

This list of Diaghilev's designers for the Ballets Russes reads like a *Who's Who* of 20th century art: Benois, Bakst and Roerich from Russia; Picasso, André Derain, Marie Laurencin, Georges Braque, Coco Chanel, Maurice Utrillo, Max Ernst, Joan Miró, Giorgio de Chirico and Georges Rouault from the fertile West.

Diaghilev worked with five choreographers during the 21 years (all of them Russian): Fokine, Nijinsky and his sister, Bronislav Nijinska, Massine, and George Balanchine.

Star dancers, star designers, star composers, star choreographers... it sounds like a recipe for success. But Diaghilev knew that art must not be subordinated to the stardom of one or other of its contributors. He was jealous that Ida Rubinstein could bring Nijinska and Massine together with Ravel and Stravinsky. But when he saw the finished product, he realized that she lacked the genius for synthesis, for fusing the separate elements into a whole. Though he described himself as having no real gift – and made light of his role, likening himself to a bartender who had invented a recipe for cocktails – those who worked with him never doubted his genius.

Diaghilev did not need stars. He called himself a 'collector of geniuses', but could build stardom himself. Great ballerinas like Pavlova and Kschessinkskaya appeared with his company, but because they preferred to be the centre of the ballet they did not stay. While he admired their artistry, he did not regret losing them. Dancers who worked with him – Nijinsky, Karsavina, Lydia Lopokova, Massine, Olga Spessivtseva – were artists who could lend their gifts interpretatively to the ballets around them, and who were prepared to direct their talents towards each ballet as a whole. Choreographers such as Nijinsky and Massine, who had little or no previous experience, were guided and coached by Diaghilev towards maturity.

Astonish me!

Diaghilev is often remembered as an impresario who liked to shock audiences and to be shocked himself. 'Etonne-moi!' ('Astonish me!') he said to Jean Cocteau. But he was all the while a man in earnest; he was concerned with tradition, not as unchanging, but as something which should be constantly renovated and developed.

When, in 1929, celebrations were proposed for the twentieth anniversary of the Ballets Russes, he said, 'I'm afraid I abhor jubilees in general and my own in particular... I wish to remain always young.' It sounds like the remark of a dandy, an aesthete. He was one. But that same year he died, an exhausted man, aged only 57. And as we look at the work of the Ballets Russes, we see how, at the expense of his own youth and vitality, he rejuvenated the whole world of art and dance.

THE GREAT COMPOSERS

Carl Orff

1895–1982

The German composer and educationalist Carl Orff wrote many ambitious choral works and a full-scale opera while still a student at the Munich Academy. But while working as a conductor and director at various opera houses, he became intrigued by music theatre; his theories on a complete synthesis between language, music and movement led him to co-found the Guntherschule. Here, Orff established his revolutionary ideas in music education, which were based on improvisation rather than on technique. His Schulwerk, a teaching guide to his methods, was eventually adopted all over the world. In 1937, Orff premiered his Carmina Burana, an exultant cantata in which he consolidated his theories to create a dramatic style. The work, analysed in the Listener's Guide, *became Orff's magnum opus. In Orff's lifetime, mankind's dreams of flight became reality;* In The Background *describes the history of aviation in the 20th century.*

Carl Orff was such an intensely private man that even his eight-volume biography revealed little about his life; he preferred to let his music speak for him. Born in Munich, Orff loved poetry, theatre and music as a child, and at 16, he had already published several compositions. He entered the Munich Academy in 1912; his impatience with the teaching methods of the Academy later helped him to formulate his Schulwerk theories. After holding conducting posts with several opera houses and a brief stint in the army, Orff met the artist and movement teacher Dorothee Günther in 1923. Together they founded the revolutionary Guntherschule for student dancers and musicians. In 1937 Orff's cantata Carmina Burana brought him great success. He continued to write in its dramatic, theatrical style, in addition to lecturing worldwide on his Schulwerk theory, until his death in 1982.

COMPOSER'S LIFE
'The gift to be simple'

Although intensely private in his personal life Carl Orff is known world-wide as the composer of Carmina Burana *and as the founder of a fresh approach to music education for children.*

Carl Orff (left) in 1936, the year before he achieved overnight recognition for his intensely dramatic work, Carmina Burana. *With this, Orff felt he had found his own musical voice and* Carmina Burana, *still his most frequently heard composition, became his Opus 1.*

Orff-Archiv

indestructable and judicious humour, her pertinent wit and her all-embracing readiness to help made her loved and remembered wherever she went'.

At the age of five Orff's own musical studies began at home where he was taught the piano by his mother, a very talented pianist, and made his first attempts at writing music on a slate. He was an imaginative child with a quick brain and although he did well at school he found that, like all his experiences of institutionalized education, it did not live up to his expectations.

It quickly became obvious early in his childhood that music was going to overtake all other interests and become Carl's chosen career. Apart from music he was interested in botany, history, languages and poetry, and probably through his early visits to theatre, developed a life-long fascination for the power of theatrical effects. Orff was taken to a marionette theatre as a child and his excited response to this was to attempt plays of his own for the puppet theatre he had been given. The plays he wrote were to be performed by himself, his sister and various school-friends. Their puppet-theatre orchestra consisted of a piano, violin, a zither, a glockenspiel and thunder effects produced by the kitchen range. Orff's own task was to 'pound the piano very loudly!'

By the time he was eight his parents had taken him to his first orchestral concert of music by Mozart and Beethoven, and he saw his first opera, Wagner's *Flying Dutchman,* when he was 13.

Archiv für Kunst und Geschichte

To most people Carl Orff is known only as the composer of the spectacular music drama, *Carmina Burana,* which shook the world with its primitive and rhythmic vitality and brought him instant fame in 1937. Yet in the midst of great acclaim Carl Orff succeeded, as always, in keeping his personal life private, insisting that it was only his work that was important. Even his own eight-volume autobiography, on which he worked from 1975 until his death in 1982, reveals little of Orff the man and concentrates instead on influences on his work and important events in his life.

Childhood in Munich

Orff was born in Munich on 10 July 1895 into an old Bavarian family with strong army connections whose interests and abilities were wide-ranging and for whom music was an essential part of everyday life.

Orff's parents, Heinrich and Paula, had known each other from childhood. His father was a career army officer while his mother had an out-and-out artistic nature. Nevertheless, she understood and supported her husband in his profession. According to Orff 'her

Orff's parents, Paula and Heinrich (above), were both talented musicians, and Orff remembered how great a part his parents' music played in his childhood. They played piano duets every afternoon or evening and on Sundays played in piano quintets or string quartets. Orff later remarked: 'everywhere there was music in which I did not take part, but which influenced me unconsciously.'

Orff was born in 1895 at 16 Maillingser Street (right) in Munich (below). As a child he spent many happy hours with both of his grandfathers, one of whom was an historian. Grandfather Koestler delighted in taking his grandson for walks through Munich, all the while providing a lively chronicle of local history.

When he was six Orff was taken to a marionette theatre (below right). This first theatrical experience was never forgotten and inspired him, three years later, to write plays with music for his own puppet theatre. These were performed with the help of his sister and various friends.

Orff-Archiv

The only problems he ever encountered in his formal musical studies were caused by his feelings towards the academic approach of his teachers. Orff showed too much independence of spirit to be able to accept without question the rigid academic methods of his instrumental teachers. He was much more eager to play his own improvisations and work out his own route to keyboard mastery than to tackle the tedious Czerny studies from the curriculum. When later Orff came to consider education in music, he remembered his own frustrations, and tried to provide a method of teaching which would not kill enthusiasm by drudgery. All his life he hated piano practice and was the first to admit that his performances were more remarkable for their character and interpretative skill than for technical wizardry.

By the time he was 15 Orff had produced a steady stream of song lyrics which he set to music with his mother's help. In 1911, at the age of 16, Orff first had some of his songs published, but even by this time had abandoned his own poetry in favour of German literature, mostly setting poems by the nineteenth-century poets: Hölderlin, Munchausen, Heine, Nietzsche and others. Orff's instinctive belief that music should serve poetry became stronger as he grew older.

Student at the Academy

He was accepted as a student at the Munich Academy of Music in 1912. His principal teacher was Beer-Walbrunn, greatly respected in his day, but strictly academic and traditional in his approach, and Orff could not win his sympathy for his approach to composition. However, after such a creative childhood it seems that the bones of his artistic personality were set and there was not much that the Academy could do to fracture them. Certainly he was as productive as ever during these student years, writing further songs and larger scale works, even completing an opera. Entitled *Gisei,* it was a romantic adaptation of a Japanese play and its 'fin de siecle' sound shows how much Orff had been studying the music of Debussy, although the orchestral forces announce the characteristic Orff in maturity, calling for an extensive battery of percussion, including a thunder sheet, wind machine, glass harmonica and two harps, over and

Archiv für Kunst und Geschichte

above the conventional instruments. Orff even
included an extra on-stage orchestra and an off-stage
choir! It was certainly an ambitious project and,
although a student work, shows how he was
beginning to assemble the brilliant palette of sound
colour he would draw on richly in years to come.

In 1914, although he had graduated from the
Munich Academy, Orff took lessons to improve his
piano technique with Hermann Zilcher. In 1916 he
took up the post of conductor and music director at
the Munich Kammerspiele, where he worked under
the direction of Falckenberg, famous for his productions of Shakespeare, Wedekind and Strindberg.
In 1917 he was conscripted to serve in the First
Bavarian Field Regiment, but was later invalided out
of the army following an incident when he was
buried in a dugout during an attack on the Eastern
Front. After the war he became music director and
conductor at Mannheim, then Darmstadt opera
houses.

Finding his musical voice

The importance of this period in Orff's life was to
show in his own theatrical works some twenty years
later, but it was at this time that he became
convinced that the way forward for him lay through
the combination of language, music and movement.
Although the sonatas and symphonies of nineteenth-
century romantic composers provided him with his
early inspiration, when it came to finding his own
musical language Orff felt they had nothing to offer.

Consequently, in 1919, Orff gave up his opera
posts and concentrated on study and composition.
He also taught a few hours a week and conducted the
Munich Bach Choir.

His private life took on a new shape in 1920 when
he married Alice Solscher. Their only child – a
daughter – Godela, was born in 1921. Orff
subsequently married Gertrud Willert in 1939; Luise
Rinser in 1954, and finally, in 1960, Liselotte
Schmitz, now his widow. Orff was intensely protec-
tive of his private life and little is known of the
personal details behind the bare facts of his marriages.

To help him in his search for a vital new style of
music theatre Orff needed to find fresh influences. He
had always been interested in contemporary culture
and particularly intrigued by the lugubrious nightmare world of the 'expressionists'; the philosophical
writings of Werfel and Nietzsche, the turbulent dis-
sonant music of Schoenberg and especially the operas
Salome and *Elektra* of Richard Strauss. But Orff felt
that many modern composers were going up blind
alleys and that the atonal music they produced was
not for him. Following the advice of Curt Sachs, an
eminent musicologist, who felt that the theatre was
Orff's metier and that he should study the first great
musical dramatist, Monteverdi, Orff became excited
by the music of Renaissance Italy – Palestrina, Roland
de Lassus, Gabrieli, and above all, Monteverdi. Orff
spent hours working on versions of Monteverdi's
operas, especially *Orfeo,* the best known of them all,
which he re-worked many times, leaving much of the
old instrumentation intact.

Orff also became interested in dance in general,
and in particular in the work of Mary Wigman and
Dorothee Günther, both of whom had studied with
Jacques Dalcroze. Dalcroze, some 30 years older
than Orff, had devised a system of movement to
music which allowed dancers to express themselves
through improvisation. Of Mary Wigman Orff wrote:

In 1912 Orff was accepted as a student at the Munich Academy. One of the large-scale works he attempted was an opera entitled Gisei, *a romantic adaptation of a Japanese play. A fashionable choice of subject, given the fascination with all things oriental (right) that prevailed in the early twentieth century, the work also reflected Debussy's influence on Orff.*

Orff's first published musical works were his own song lyrics. Soon after their publication in 1911, when he was 16, he abandoned his own poetry in favour of that of many 19th-century German poets, including Heinrich Heine (below).

Orff became interested in the relationship between music and movement through the work of Mary Wigman, a dancer whose style he described as 'elemental'. She had studied movement and dance with the innovatory Emile-Jacques Dalcroze (left) and Rudoph von Laban.

In 1923 Orff met Dorothee Günther, an artist and movement teacher, who had developed her own ideas on movement. Her first collaboration with Orff was as the librettist for his arrangement of Monteverdi's opera Orfeo (title page below).

The art of Mary Wigman was very significant for me and my later work. All her dances were animated by an unprecedented musicality. She could make music with her body and transform music into corporeality. I felt that her dancing was elemental. I too was searching for the elemental, for elemental music.

He met Dorothee Günther in 1923 through mutual friends, and they soon found they had much in common. She was an artist whose experiences in life-drawing classes made her realize that many people found simple movement complicated and awkward. She became obsessed with the idea of creating a form of movement education. She had turned to the then-new form of physical education, Mensendieck Gymnastics, and also came to know the work of Dalcroze and Laban.

Dorothee Günther gave courses and lectures on her ideas and it was these that brought her to Munich in 1923. Orff played her some of his sketches for his arrangement of Monteverdi's *Orfeo* and described his vain attempts with experienced librettists to make a new and free German text. She offered to take this on and brought the task to a successful conclusion.

In 1924 Orff was co-founder with Dorothee Günther of the Güntherschule. At the School (below) student teachers of movement were themselves taught Orff's fresh approach to music education.

The Güntherschule

Together in 1924 they founded the Güntherschule for young student dancers and musicians where they could realize their ideas about music and dance education. Because of his own unsatisfactory early experiences with music teachers Orff had become an outspoken critic of the unimaginative methods that were currently being employed. With the Güntherschule established he now had an ideal medium in which to carry out artistic and educational research. In the years that followed, he developed the approach to music called Orff-Schulwerk, (or 'Music for Children'), designed to help children to discover their own musicality through improvisation in music and movement. The basic idea was that pupils should seek out the musician inside themselves, by themselves, rather than by a conscious learning or teaching process. Orff had long felt that one of the barriers to the vivid expressive powers of little children was traditional instrumental teaching. The long years of study and scale practice that were a necessary prelude to playing 'real music' quickly killed the enthusiasm of many genuinely musical children. Orff believed that the solution to the problem of the technical barrier lay in using instruments that are easy to play

satisfyingly well with the minimum of initial learning. The instruments he advocated, which became known as 'Orff Instruments', were xylophones, metallophones and glockenspiels adapted for children's use; all kinds of drums; shaken instruments, such as maracas and tambourines; woodblocks, claves, triangles, cymbals, recorders, bass string instruments and also plucked strings.

Essentially Orff wrote his Schulwerk for use locally in Bavaria, never dreaming that it would arouse the world-wide interest it did. The experience gained at the Güntherschule encouraged him to plan for the introduction of these ideas into schools. But because of the political situation the plans did not come to fruition. The Güntherschule itself was compulsorily closed in 1944 by the Nazi Area Commander for the city of Munich, and was eventually destroyed in a bombing raid. It was much later, in 1948, when a gramophone record of the dance music of the Güntherschule was discovered, that the Bavarian radio programmes were broadcast which eventually led to the adoption of Orff's Schulwerk in Germany, and then throughout the world.

No doubt the reasons for the success of Orff-Schulwerk had much to do with the fact that its creator was neither an educational theorist nor a

The premiére in 1937 of **Carmina Burana** *in Frankfurt am Main (the original set is shown above) brought Orff great acclaim and marked the establishment of his own musical style. The source of the work was a collection of medieval lyrics (a manuscript page, right) from the monastery of Benediktbeuren. Although* **Carmina Burana** *is now usually performed as a choral work in the concert hall, it was originally intended for presentation in the theatre with ballet.*

In 1960 Orff married his fourth wife, Liselotte Schmitz (below). Orff spent the last years of his life, from 1975 to 1982, working on the eight volume documentation of his life and work. Frau Orff, now his widow, is closely involved with the running of the Orff-Archiv in Diessen am Ammersee, near Munich.

schoolmaster but a creative artist who was sincerely trying to break down barriers between art and education.

Although much occupied with the Güntherschule and Orff-Schulwerk Orff continued to search for his own musical language. Finally, with *Carmina Burana,* which became his opus 1, he felt he had found his voice, and decided to withdraw all previous work. A few of his earlier choral works have now been republished and are available in English translations. For the rest of his creative life all his work was specifically for the theatre. He felt that through these works for the theatre he had reconciled music with language in the way the Greeks had. For him music was the unity of sound, language and movement.

Orff did not bask in the success of the 'Carmina Burana' for long. The first of its successors – *'Der Mond'* (The Moon) – an allegory from Grimm's fairy tales about Heaven and Earth and the World of the Dead was performed in 1939. Folk tales provided the inspiration for one or two subsequent works including *Die Kluge* (The Clever Girl), first performed in 1943.

Although folklore was the source for *Die Bernaurin* (The woman from Bernau) first produced in Stuttgart in 1947 Orff took a new direction. His stage directions called for a huge cast of actors and singers which he used as commentators on the action, like the chorus in a Greek tragedy.

He carried the classical parallel further in his next music drama by using a real Greek tragedy, Sophocles' *Antigone* – in a version by the poet Hölderlin. Of *Antigone* he said: 'It is not a work for the opera repertoire, it is a ceremonial, a cult work. I consider my work as merely a rendering of Sophocles' play for our time; his is the significant contribution, not mine. Behind him lies a whole world.' At the same time as he was writing and producing his theatre work Orff was director of a master-class in composition at the Munich Academy.

Between 1950 and 1954 the music publisher Schott published the five German volumes of Orff-Schulwerk. English and Canadian editions of the work were prepared and published over a number of years, and in 1961, relinquishing his Munich teaching post, he founded the official training centre for Orff-Schulwerk at the Mozarteum in Salzberg.

In 1953 children from the school gave demonstrations of their work at an International Conference of Music School Directors, and this marks the beginning of the world-wide appeal of Orff-Schulwerk.

During the 1960s Orff travelled extensively, giving lectures on Orff-Schulwerk in Japan, Canada, Portugal, Egypt and Senegal. In 1972 he was awarded an Honorary Doctorate by Munich University, and a medal from the state was for services in the field of culture and politics. In 1973 his last work *A play about the end of time, The Vigil,* was performed in Salzburg.

Carl Orff died in Munich on 29th March 1982, a respected figure. In the years of his old age many academic honours had been conferred on him in recognition of his life's achievement, perhaps paradoxically, for one so anti-academic and for one whose music was non-intellectual almost to the point of primitivism. But it will surely always be enjoyed as the legacy of a man who, as one musicologist put it, 'had the gift to be simple'.

Carmina Burana

Carl Orff's colourful cantata **Carmina Burana,** *with its pounding rhythms, medieval symbolism and robust humour, has proved to be one of the 20th century's most enduringly popular choral works.*

When the *Carmina Burana* received its première in Frankfurt on 6 June 1937, it proved to be the culmination, and triumphal vindication, of Orff's ideas on music and theatre. Combining the theatricality of a medieval procession with simple, powerful orchestration, the *Carmina* is the perfect marriage of music and stage that Orff had been seeking for over 20 years. For Orff, it was so successful that it made all his previous work superfluous: 'With *Carmina Burana,* my collected works begin.'

Orff's burning interest in musical theatre may date back to 1915-17, when he was conducting the orchestra of the Munich Kammerspiele theatre. Here, he was introduced to the revolutionary expressionist style of theatre fostered by the plays of people like Bertolt Brecht, and no doubt formed his own ideas on the potential of theatre. In the 1920s, these ideas were focused by his growing fascination with the Renaissance masters of music — Monteverdi especially — and with the triumphal processions, masques and dances of that period.

Gradually, Orff moved towards his own peculiar concept of theatre, blending the spectacle of the Renaissance pageant with the experimental freedom of modern drama. Orff saw the theatre as a place where the modern audience should be delighted by sound, movement and colour yet be presented with concepts and ideas rather than simple narratives.

Interestingly, it was Orff's fascination with the Renasissance and Middle Ages that led to the idea for the *Carmina Burana.* The *Carmina Burana* was actually a collection of almost 200 medieval poems and songs discovered in the library of the Benedictine monastery of Beuren near Munich in 1803 — the title was given to them by Joseph Schmeller who edited the collection in 1847. The poems are a wonderful mixture of verses by monks and lyrics by goliards (wandering scholar minstrels). Some are humorous; some are sad; some are bawdy; some Christian and some Pagan. But all are very human.

For his cantata, Orff took about 20 of these poems and arranged them into '*Cantiones profanae cantoribus et cantandae comitantibus instrumentis atque imaginibus magicis,*' which means 'profane songs for soloists and choruses, accompanied by instruments and magic images'.

The whole piece is shot through with medieval symbolism, and the potent medieval theme of the Wheel of Fortune, ever-turning, bringing good luck and bad luck, frames the cantata. The *Carmina* both begins and ends with an address to the goddess Fortuna, the ruler of the world, who makes men and women and breaks them. The Wheel of Fortune rolls through the three sections of the piece, as men and women encounter the natural pleasures of life — nature (*Primo vere* and *Uf dem anger),* eating and drinking *(In taberna),* and love (*Cour d'Amours).*

Later in his life, Orff joined two other theatrical pieces to the *Carmina Burana* to create a new work. His mini-opera *Catulli Carmina,* on the trials and tribulations of the love life of the Roman poet Catullus, was produced in Leipzig in 1943. Then in 1953 at Milan, the third and final part, *Trionfo di Afrodite* (the Triumph of Aphrodite, goddess of love), was performed. Together, the three works are known simply as *Trionfi.* But it is the *Carmina Burana* alone which is best known and loved.

Programme notes

Carmina Burana is a scenic cantata and presents a series of pictures set like pieces of a stained-glass window in a strong dark frame — the dark frame is the Wheel of Fortune motif. The songs are grouped thematically to deal with three major aspects of human life. The driving rhythms and clear song structures help to guide the listener through the three sections: spring and the out-of-doors, the tavern, and the court of love. The piece demands a large orchestra with a sizeable percussion section, and the wide variety of orchestral colouring still continues to startle audiences today.

Fortuna imperatrix mundi

The cantata opens with a presentation of Fortuna, empress of the world — the Fateful goddess who raises men up and sinks them down. She is presented in the traditional guise as the goddess who controls our fate, often with gleeful malice.

O Fortuna velut luna, the first song, is a resounding choral address to the wayward goddess accompanied by a great crash on the timpani and piano. It is marked *Pesante* ('with weight') and seems to symbolise the great Wheel of Fortune rolling forward:

Hieronymus Bosch 'The Garden of Earthly Delights.' Prado, Madrid. Joachim Blauel/Artothek

The idea for Carmina Burana (original autograph score, above) sprang from Orff's fascination with the Middle Ages and Man's profane nature – as vividly portrayed in The Garden of Earthly Delights by Hieronymus Bosch (left). This main theme is symbolically 'framed' by the ever-turning Wheel of Fortune (below) which governs Man's fate.

Example 1

♩ = 60 Pesante

O For—tu—na ve—lut Lu—na

After this explosive entry, the rhythm quickens, but the chorus becomes much quieter and only the pounding strings and woodwind accompaniment are left to echo the turning of the Wheel. When the chorus cry out their final complaint at the vagaries of fate at full voice, the trombones and trumpets lend to the instrumental coda a sustained note of anguish.

The rotating rhythm of the great wheel is sustained throughout the second song, *Fortuna plango vulnera* although slightly quicker. But here a poet laments his fate at the hands of the goddess. The chorus is begun by the bass, but the rest of the chorus gradually joins in, accompanied by furious whirring strings and a startling fanfare figure on trumpets and then horns. With the malice of Fortune firmly established, Orff launches into the first of the three aspects of human life.

I Primo vere

With three odd bird-like calls on flutes, oboes, and percussion, Nature awakens. The first song of Spring, *Veris leta facies*, begins, and is repeated. Sustained chords on the horn, trombone and piano lead into an undulating chorus of altos, tenors and basses. The atmosphere is one of mystery, magic and nocturnal silence. All three stanzas end with a soft choral exclamation on the syllable Ah! – like a prolonged choral sigh.

A flute and glockenspiel give another bird-call before the baritone soloist sings of the healing power of the sun in a song called *Omnia sol temperat*. The singer's phrases are uttered softly, like those of the preceding chorus, but the impetus seems greater as his words tumble over each other. His intense delivery continues through all three verses over a shimmering instrumental background until a sustained note on the contrabassoon closes the song.

A sparkling chorus, *Ecce gratum*, welcomes the spring and summer with good humour, and tenors begin a new song. As the sopranos join in, the texture thickens and the pace quickens. After an exuberant exchange between tenors and chorus the verse ends with a great choral cry. The following verses balance tenors against basses before the full chorus joins in, powered along by cymbals and gong.

On the green

From now on, the work becomes much more specific and pictorial, as a quick little Bavarian dance for strings, introduced by solemn brass chords and a drum roll, paints a picture of people dancing on the green.

Soon the full chorus are describing the beauty of the woodlands in a song called *Floret silva*. Sopranos and altos then ask where their beloved has gone. The tenors

David Teniers 'Tavern Scene with Dancing Peasant Couple' Bayerische Staatsgemälde Samlungen/Joachim Blauel/Artothek

In the section entitled 'On the Green', Orff introduces a human element into the theme for the first time with a series of dances – some formal, others light-hearted, like this peasant dance (below), but all are a joyful celebration of life.

The central part of the Carmina Burana paints a picture of a colourful tavern scene (above), with the music rapidly changing in mood from the gloomy self-pity of one solitary singer to rowdy convivial frivolity.

Peter Breugel 'Dance of the Peasants' Uffizi, Florence. Scala

reply that he has ridden away and the rhythm of their reply suggests a galloping steed.

Example 2

Their voices fade away in the distance with a far-away horn call. The women lament being left alone, first in Latin, then in medieval German.

But the melancholy mood is soon dispelled as sopranos sing of buying make-up and attracting men in a joyful chorus accompanied by bells. During the slower section the full chorus can be heard humming with pleasure, to a flute accompaniment.

The women emerge with a stately and formal dance, with tuba and strings punctuated by melancholy brass fanfares. But a much livelier dance on *pizzicato* (plucked) strings soon breaks out and there begins a chorus of primitive and increasing intensity. Girls who dance hoping to find a man for the summer are mocked and their song reaches a stirring climax before altos softly seduce the girls with a lovely melody, echoed by a wandering solo flute. The lively dance chorus returns and ends with a mocking shout.

A very fast staccato fanfare begins the last dance in this section. Trumpets and

Understanding music: Musical wit

Not all classical music is written in a deadly serious vein. Indeed, many great composers have introduced a rich humour into their works in the form of musical wit.

Two of the most common forms of musical wit are the related areas *parody* and *pastiche,* both of which are used to mimic the work or style of another composer for jocular effect. Pastiche, though, differs slightly from parody in that it presents a collection of passages, either borrowed directly or written in imitation, usually from the works of more than two composers. Deriving from the Italian term *pasticcio* (hotchpotch), pastiche was a common feature of 18th-century Italian opera. But both before and since then there have been many musical examples which reveal the amusing side of composition.

Parody in the satirical sense is the essence of Mozart's *A Musical Joke* – perhaps the best known of all parodies. In this he mocks the constructional rigidities of lesser composers and the playing of inexpert musicians. Beethoven, too, obviously found the latter point amusing for he 'sends-up' village musicians by the 'mistimed' bassoon entries in the 'Pastoral Symphony'.

Opera, with its exotic conventions, is particularly susceptible to parody. The high drama and musical virtuosity with which the heroines in Mozart's *Cosi fan tutte* protest a fidelity that does not last one day, is a famous example – and even parodies Mozart's own heroic style. In Wagner's comedy, *Die Meistersinger von Nürenberg,* the pedantry of the composer's critics is lampooned in the character of Sixtus Bechmesser, whose unmusical wooing of the heroine Eva is laughably (some feel, cruelly) unsuccessful. One of the most extended parodies in opera occurs in Britten's *A Midsummer Night's Dream.* Just as Shakespeare parodies the absurdities of the theatre in the rustic's play of the last act, so Britten in his music employs various operatic styles from the past, including a witty and touching Donizettian Thisbe who dies to a florid vocal cadenza.

Parody is also a useful way of pricking pomposity, by quoting another composer's theme in a ludicrously inappropriate context. Britten does this in *Albert Herring,* when the gullible young hero drinks his lemonade secretly laced with rum while the orchestra quotes Wagner's *Tristan und Isolde.* Such an effect works on several levels: most obviously there is the joke itself – a harmless prank accompanied by music associated with a love potion and an ensuing tragedy. But there is also a subtle compliment paid to the composer of the theme quoted, for it is assumed that the theme is a celebrated one – no point quoting unknown music. Also, the audience is flattered since the composer assumes they will recognize the quote.

Parody is also a useful tool for the more popular forms of music to poke fun at serious genres. Thus the superserious 16th-century madrigal is mocked in the frottolas and canzonas of the day, and the huge success of Gay's *The Beggar's Opera,* with its popular tunes, forced Handel's operas off the London stage. French piano music is especially rich in parody. There are Satie's satires, Ravel's pieces 'in the manner of Borodin and Chabrier (once called 'a parody of Chabrier parodying Gounod') and Debussy's *Golliwog's Cakewalk* which quotes *Tristan und Isolde* (obviously a favourite target). Usually such quotations are in the spirit of affectionate mockery. Composers do not usually parody what they do not like. But there are examples of a more barbed attitude. Schoenberg's three 'satires' for chorus have texts by the composer himself and the second of them is an attack on Stravinsky, who is called 'little Modernsky'. The piece is called 'Many-sidedness' in reference to Stravinsky's various styles and to the structure of the piece itself. This may be sung backwards, by turning the page upside down and starting at the end, to produce exactly the same piece.

Not all musical attacks are so elaborate, though. Bartók in his *Concerto for Orchestra,* decided to express his contempt for the theme Shostakovich uses in his 'Leningrad' symphony to depict the approach of the Nazis by quoting it and then having the whole orchestra deride it.

Of course, there are many other ways in which music may draw on its own past without parodying it. Stravinsky's neo-classical pieces do so, as do sets of variety based on another composer's theme, such as the many 'Paganini' variations; or transcriptions such as Liszt made for the orchestra of Schubert's songs and for the piano of Beethoven's symphonies. But even variations can have a sting in their tail. Beethoven was one of the many composers approached by the publisher Diabelli to contribute a variation each on a waltz theme of Diabelli's own composition. Perhaps out of pique, Beethoven made the banal tune yield 33 variations and a tremendous fugue, effortlessly affirming his superiority over his contemporaries.

The section 'In the Court of Love' reaches an erotic climax with the song 'Veni, veni, venias' as men and women are united in an orgiastic frenzy. It is a celebration of physical love more daring even than the mood of the painting above.

trombones hammer out the tune before the chorus enters singing in a contrasting slow, pounding rhythm. In this song, the poet offers to give up the whole world (if it were his) to lie with the Queen of England! The fanfare returns and the chorus give a final joyful shout.

II In the tavern

The exuberant joy of the last chorus would seem to lead naturally into drinking songs. But Orff has chosen his first 'tavern' song from amongst the collection's gloomiest lyrics. The baritone soloist sings of 'seething with boiling rage' and of the bitter failure of his life. In the central section his misery unfolds even further as the singer compares himself to a ship without a pilot, or an aimless bird. As his list of depravity and self-pity draws to a close, brass join the strings to end with a mighty orchestral thump. The intensity of this dramatic piece is in sharp contrast with the comic lament of a roasting swan that follows.

It concerns a swan slowly roasting on a

grotesque orchestration.

In the next song, also comic, a baritone declaims his verse in an ecclesiastical style. His mock litany proclaims him to be the Abbot of Cucany who robs anyone he meets of their wealth by gambling. His victims' cries are depicted in the male chorus' shout of *Wafna!* – a doleful word roughly the equivalent of 'Alas!'

The final song of the section, *In taberna quando sumus,* is a pulsating description of the life of the tavern crowd. The verses are muttered, depicting the manic mumbling in the background of the inn. Occasionally, bursts of sound spring up before the original rhythm returns. Attention centres more and more on the subject of he who drinks, *Bibit,* and this word is repeated again and again as the pace and volume increase together. At the height of the uproar, the chorus call out their toast of *Io!* many times in quick succession. Once again, Orff delays the final call by a sustained orchestral passage at the end of the song.

A chorus of children's voices introduces the theme of love. They sing of Cupid, who along with Venus (below) is the mythical guardian of lovers everywhere.

III The court of love

The transition to the world of courtly love is dramatic. The section opens with a slow introduction of sustained chords. A children's chorus is introduced by a lyrical woodwind section. They sing of the god of love who flies everywhere and sees lovers unite.

Darker woodwind lead into the second section in which the soprano coyly complains of being alone. The children comment briefly on her unhappiness. The lovely balance between children and soprano, with the beautiful floating accompaniment, make this one of the most appealing pieces in the whole cantata.

A tender, haunting song with a very high baritone melody called *Dies nox et omnia* (Day, night and all) is matched by the soprano's plaintive song which follows. Over soft strings, flutes, horns, glockenspiel and celesta, she sings of a shy girl in a red dress, longing for love.

The rhythm accelerates as the baritone praises his beloved with increasing passion and prays 'to undo the chains of her virginity'. His three verses are each followed by a broken chorus which ends in a crescendo of sexual intensity. First the tenors and basses repeat his melodic line;

spit. A melancholy meandering clarinet describes the swan; flutes and bassoons seem to depict the turning spit. The verses are sung by a tenor at falsetto range. In the first verse, he fondly remembers his beauty before he was put on the spit; in the second verse he describes his turning on the spit; and in the third verse he is in the serving dish and surrounded by biting teeth! Hungry baritones round off each verse with a chorus describing the swan's roasted condition with great relish. A trombone adds comic touches to the

'Venus & Cupid' Flanders 16thC. Bulloz

then the women begin the teasing refrain, *Manda liet.* The men repeat their words fiercely. The women speed up their words until they scream *niet* (not) several times against an orchestral climax.

An explicit chorus for solo men called *Si puer cum puellula* (If a boy is with a girl) follows. The poem describes a scientific experiment: place a young girl and a young boy alone in a little room and what happens? The chorus twice call out *Felix coniunctio!* in celebration of sexual union.

Soon the women are calling the men to come *(Veni, veni, venias),* and the men respond with the same cry. The orchestra uses triangle, drums and cymbals to punctuate their growing orgiastic frenzy. The entire chorus is shouting in ecstacy when suddenly the mood changes.

With tender melody accompanied by the sound of delicate strings and flute, a sole soprano sings with a lyric intensity in

The burning intensity of the 'Court of Love' section finally subsides into an ordered more gentle expression of the higher ideals of love and marriage (below) where women are objects of worship.

wonderful contrast to the surrounding dramatic choruses.

In these two verses, the girl hesitates between physical love and chastity. Her problem is still unresolved when the chorus bursts into a passionate exposition of burning love, announced by a barrage of percussive instruments. The refrain is first given by the baritone solo; then by the soprano accompanied by the children's chorus. Finally, the entire chorus joins in a refrain which leads without resolution into the next song.

In a very short, but most beautiful section for the soprano, called Dulcissime, she yields herself to her sweet lover, *con abbandono* (with abandon).

Her falling, almost oriental sounding *melisma* (an extended run of notes on a single syllable) symbolizes her submission to her lover and the eternal union of male and female.

Blaniflor et Helena
Without a break, the chorus proceeds to the final part of The Court of Love section with a marriage song of heroic dimensions for the young man and woman called *Ave formosissima.* This is a formal procession with ever denser orchestration which reintroduces the chivalric ideal of service to women and the purity of love. The pagan song ends with a call to the goddess Venus, *Venus generosa,* the goddess of

Johann Georg Platzer 'Summer' Victoria & Albert Museum

love. The repeated cry is accentuated by tam-tam drum beats as the crescendo builds to Orff's last surprise.

The call to the goddess returns the music suddenly to the beginning of the cantata and the grim view of Fortune. Perhaps Venus and Fortuna are the same deity? In any case, Orff seems to imply that human love and the beauty of nature exist despite the surrounding world and its brutality and ugliness. Once again this chorus sinks to a quiet restatement of the complaint against Fortune after the dynamic opening. Again at the third and final verse, the crescendo begins to build until the cantata ends with a blazing aural panorama.

The medieval atmosphere is so essential to Carmina Burana *that it is retained even in the more avant-garde modern stagings of the work – as in this set design for a 1968 Berlin Opera production, where a backdrop of gothic-style architecture is used to symbolize the work's medieval roots.*

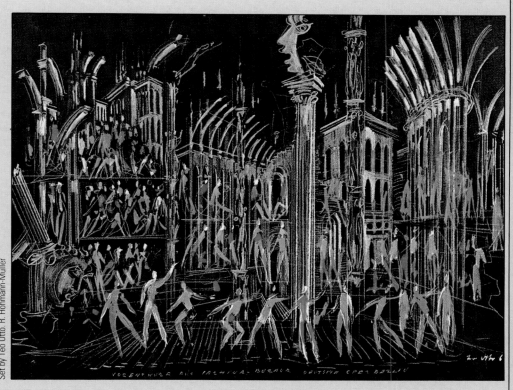

Set by Teo Otto: R. Höhmann-Müller

Great interpreters

Phonogram International

Herbert Kegel (above).

Leipzig Symphony Orchestra & Radio Chorus
The Leipzig Symphony Orchestra arose out of a combination of two orchestras, the Leipzig Philharmonic and the Leipzig Gewandhaus, for special concert series, as early as 1915. These were part of a general plan for adult education. In 1924, with the rapid spread of radio, the Mitteldeutsche Rundfunk AG was founded, and the Leipzig Symphony Orchestra became the radio station's resident orchestra. Its first conductor was Alfred Sendrey, and he stayed with the orchestra until 1932.

Choral performances were given with the aid of the Arbeiter-Sängerband. From 1930 onwards, the orchestra gave public concerts and built up a solid reputation. It was led during 1931 to 33 by Carl Schuricht before the orchestra, consistent with all other cultural organisations across Germany, became subject to direct interference and harassment from the new Nazi government. In 1933 Schuricht finally

resigned, and during that year the S.S. actually arrested some orchestra members in mid-rehearsal. By 1934 no Jewish members remained in the orchestra, and it was led from then until 1939 by Hans Weisbach.

After the devastation of the war, the division of Germany, and the establishment of the communist government, the orchestra was revived with a handful of players. In 1960 Herbert Kegel became chief conductor.

In 1947 a radio choir was formed, followed in 1948 by a youth choir. Kegel also led this choir from 1953 to 1960.

Herbert Kegel (conductor)
Kegel was born in Dresden in 1920, and completed his music studies at the school of the Saxon State Orchestra there before World War II. After a period in Pirna, he moved to Leipzig, where he became the conductor of the Radio Choir in 1953 then its music director in 1958. In 1960 he became chief conductor of the Radio Orchestra, holding that post uninterrupted until 1977, when he became chief conductor of the Dresden Symphony Orchestra. During his long tenure at Leipzig he made many recordings for the state record company, most of which have not been released in the West.

His repertoire, like the orchestra's, is vast, and they have completed many concert and recording programmes. These range from Handel and Bach, through the great 19th-century composers, up to Stravinsky, Dessau, Hans Werner Henze and even Britten. He is today one of Eastern Europe's most distinguished representatives in classical music.

FURTHER LISTENING

Catulli Carmina
The song of Catullus is the second work in Orff's *Trionfi* trilogy, the first of which is the *Carmina Burana*. Inspired by the love poetry of the Roman poet Catullus, it details his miserable love affair with his girl, Lesbia, in a series of solo and choral interludes. Although on a smaller scale the work is as dramatic as its predecessor. Also like *Carmina Burana*, it fully merits separate performance from the other two acts, and is most often heard this way.

Die Kluge
Die Kluge (The Clever Girl) approaches opera in its conception, though, as is usual with Orff, he carefully avoids lush arias or over-inflated plots. The music, though lyrical and affecting, is interspersed with long stretches of recitative. Based on a Grimm fairy tale, it incorporates folk-like melodies and a simple, attractive jauntiness into the music in general. The orchestral colour and the story's whimsical comedy are a sharp contrast to a lot of Orff's later writing.

Antigone
In this stage play with music, the music employed returns to the simplest of changes and rhythmic speech, as is consistent with an accompaniment to a Sophoclean tragedy. Orff is careful to keep the music subservient at all times to the story, and, as such, there is little melody — the instruments being confined mainly to percussive roles. All rests with the voice and words, and when well performed provides a powerful experience.

76

IN THE BACKGROUND

'Flying Machines'

After the first tentative powered aircraft flights in the opening years of the 20th century, it took man less than 60 years to conquer the skies, making the dream of flight a reality.

On 17 December 1903, near Kitty Hawk, North Carolina, USA, a centuries-old dream at last came true: on Kill Devil Hill man rose from the face of the earth and, for the first time, flew in controlled, powered flight. On that historic occasion, the bicycle manufacturers Orville and Wilbur Wright made four short flights in their primitive airplane, Flyer I – the first lasting just 12 seconds, the last almost one minute. The road to conquest of the skies in heavier-than-air machines had begun.

Despite the achievement, the event passed almost unnoticed; the American press virtually ignored it. To the great majority of people what little news they received was largely met with disbelief. Few realised that the fundamental problems of powered flight had at last been solved. Fewer still understood how it had been achieved. Orville and Wilbur Wright appeared to be just two more in a long line of crazed lunatics who had tried to reach for the sky. And the history of previous attempts had been rich in catastrophe and spectacular failure.

Getting off the ground
The idea, and indeed reality, of flight was not new. Like all scientific and technological advance, the Wrights' achievement was built on the work of many previous experiments. As early as 1783 the Montgolfier Brothers, in France, had made the first successful balloon flights and by the early 20th century ballooning was well established across the world. But balloons were prey to wind and weather and aviators had no real control over their craft. So the search for controlled, sustained flight went on as it had done over the centuries.

The idea of heavier-than-air flight dates far back in history. In the late 15th century, for example, Leonardo da Vinci constructed small model 'flying' craft – some resembling helicopters, others designed with flapping, bird-like wings. But despite Leonardo's genius, none of his designs was practicable as he, like so many that followed him, had not grasped the principles of flight. In fact it was the attempts to imitate bird flight – a practical impossibility for man – that side-tracked inventors for hundreds of years.

Experiments with gliders showed the real way forward. Sir George Cayley, a British baronet, made model gliders from 1804 onwards and worked out some important aerodynamic principles. He even flew his coachman in a full-sized craft in 1853 – the first man-carrying aircraft flight in history. However, Cayley could go no further than gliding – he could not power his craft with a suitable engine: technology had simply not progressed sufficiently far.

The problem of finding a power plant dogged the quest for flight in the second half of the 19th century. There were experiments with steam engines: Samuel Henson's Aerial Steam Carriage of 1848, Henri Giffard's steam-powered dirigible of 1852 and Clement Ader's bat-winged Avion III monoplane. But steam power was not the answer. No steam engine could be made light enough for flight.

It was the internal combustion engine, developed for the motor car, which provided the answer. It was with such an engine, in conjunction with other innovations, that the Wright Brothers were able to make controlled, sustained flight possible. Their prototype airplanes incorporated four important features: a relatively advanced chain-driven propellor, rear rudder, aileron, and moveable, warped wings. By 1905 they were able to demonstrate their latest airplane, Flyer III, banking, turning, circling, making figures-of-eight and staying airborne for 30 minutes or more at a time. Other would-be aviators had been misled for years by the idea that a plane must be a rigid, stable design in order to fly. The Wrights' secret lay in the deliberately *unstable* structure of their Flyers. They had to be controlled in the air and *made* to fly by the skill of the pilot.

Man's dream of flight is ages old. Greek myth tells of Daedalus and Icarus who fly on home-made, bird-like wings.

Saraceni 'the Fall of Icarus' Napoli Capodimonte/Scala

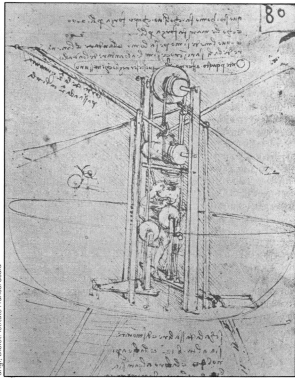

As long as 2000 years ago, children were playing with 'winged' tops – effectively, toy helicopters. These may have originated in China. An anonymous picture (far left), painted about 1460, shows the Christ-child holding just such a toy. In the 15th century, Leonardo da Vinci probably played with one long before he drew up his sketches for flying machines (one design shown left).

On 1 December 1783, shortly after the Montgolfier Brother's first-ever hot air balloon flight, Messrs Robert and Charles launched the first gas-filled balloon from the Tuilleries Gardens, Paris, and flew for two hours (left). Charles' invention proved a vast improvement on the crude hot-air balloon. But when Charles went up for a second flight, alone, his rapid ascent to 9,000ft (2,750m) frightened him so much that he never flew again. Balloons and dirigibles made flight possible, but controlled flight was still a long way off.

Public reaction

The public found it difficult to grasp that true flight had been accomplished. In 1903, long railway journeys were still something of a romantic adventure; the sailing ship had only just been wholly replaced by steamships; and the first jerky cinema films were still a novelty. Electricity, the telephone and especially the motor car were still the prerogatives of the rich. Those with the money and daring to take to the air were dubbed crazy, ungodly and (in the case of women) unladylike.

A craze for freak aircraft seized Britain in 1909-10, producing weird machines such as the circular-winged Mortimer and Vaughan 'Safety', and the Seddon which had a mass of hoops for wings. In 1910, a Californian, Professor Zerbe, built a plane with five

flights in Britain by an all-British aircraft.

By this time, the biplane design was beginning to show its superiority over others. Monoplanes had been built but with the materials then available they could barely withstand the stresses and strains of flight. A pair of biplane wings braced together by struts and wires was strong and rigid yet sufficiently light. The need for streamlining also started to be taken into account as experience of air-resistance and drag grew.

Within a decade of the Wright Brothers' first flights, major developments were taking place in European aviation. The brothers themselves made extensive lecture tours and gave flying demonstrations. Interest grew rapidly. Aeronautical research laboratories sprang up in Germany, Italy and even in Russia (which was technologically backward in many other ways). Moscow had an Aerodynamic Institute as early as 1904 and in Britain, the Netherlands and the United States, young aviation pioneers were writing their names in the annals of flying history. They included Geoffrey de Havilland, founder of the aircraft company which built the Mosquito, Tiger Moth and the Comet, the first jet air-liner; Igor Sikorsky, inventor of the four-engined aircraft and the helicopter; and Anton Fokker, creator of a whole range of war-planes.

It was the French, however, who pursued aviation science with the greatest enthusiasm. The Eiffel Laboratory was the first to have a wind tunnel for testing aircraft. By 1910, France had more aircraft engines available than any other nation, as well as being world-leaders in the science of streamlining. The French were also given to staging aviation weeks and aerial races, which promoted the new technology with a great deal of flair. The events took on a romantic image: pilots became the great daredevils of the age.

The stimulus of war

There was a more sober aspect, however, to the race for progress in aviation. The military potential of aircraft was soon recognized, so confirming the deepest fears of the Wright Brothers who had naively hoped their invention would never be used in war. Aviation units were formed within the armed forces of the United States in 1907, in Britain in 1912, with

wings staggered like a staircase. This was modest compared with models with 12, 20, 50 and even 200 wings. Zerbe's creation tripped in a pothole while dashing for take-off across Dominguez Field near Los Angeles and ended up a pile of wreckage. Most of the other fantasies similarly failed to get off the ground. Consequently it was several years before airplanes were generally accepted as anything other than novelty machines by the general public.

In the meantime, though, serious research was underway for the optimum aircraft shape and for comfortable flying conditions for the pilots. In 1903 the Wrights had flown using a posture once suggested by Leonardo da Vinci: lying flat down and rolling from side to side to keep the plane steady. Other pilots flew standing up or perched precariously on a girder, as in Alliott Verdon Roe's Bull's Eye Avroplane of 1909. This had three wings in front and a matching triple tailplane, all of them wrapped in brown paper. Nevertheless, for all its strange appearance, the Avroplane (backed ironically by a maker of men's suspenders) was of feasible design and, in July 1909, made the first official powered

Over the years, all manner of means had been tried to defy gravity (above). By 1894, such genuine strides had been made in aerodynamics that Octave Chanute (right) was able to publish a book entitled **Progress in Flying Machines.** *A builder, pilot and collector of gliders, Chanute's greatest contribution was perhaps the inspiration his book gave to Wilbur and Orville Wright.*

serious, bloody business of war. The idea of killing a pilot, enemy or no, was very bad form. But this chivalrous phase was quickly over. On 15th August 1914, Reuter's correspondent reported, '... a French aeroplane yesterday encountered an enemy aeroplane. The French pilot chased the German, firing with a Browning (machine gun). The German aviator did not reply, but fled.'

Two months later, the first aircraft to be shot down was a German Aviatik reconnaissance plane which burst into flames when riddled with bullets from ground fire and crashed in full view of opposing ground troops. The age of aerial warfare had begun in earnest.

World War I inevitably provided a forcing ground for aviation. It tested the sturdiness and nimbleness of aircraft in dog-fight combat where pilots flew close enough to exchange gunfire with handguns, or endeavoured to knock each other out of the sky with bricks dangling below their planes. To begin with the bombs they carried were scarcely more than hand-grenades, but could be dropped with deadly accuracy by the pilot leaning out of the cockpit. Quite soon, on-board machine guns were synchronized to fire between the blades of a spinning propellor. By the end of the War, planes were covering considerable distances in order to drop a bomb-load, and aero-engines had been thoroughly tested and improved accordingly. In only four years, the airplane had been changed from an under-powered, flimsy box-kite into a punchy, resilient fighting machine, and out of war-hardened pilots was forged a new breed of adventurer.

Flyer I *(above), built by the Wright Brothers (left), became the world's first successful airplane when Orville Wright made three short flights near Kitty Hawk on 17th December 1903. Just six years later, flying had progressed so fast that Blériot was able to fly the English Channel (below) in his home-made monoplane.*

the idea in mind of aerial reconnaissance. And in 1911, the Italian Aviation Battalion first proved airplanes' reconnaissance role in combat during the war between Italy and Turkey. On 23rd October 1911, the Italian Battalion's commander, Captain Carlo Piazza, flew a Bleriot XI monoplane on the first wartime mission. Three days later, Piazza directed ship- and shore-based artillery at the battle of Scaria-Scarat, and on 1st November made the first air raid when he dropped four bombs on Turkish positions.

More alarming than these first offensive flights were the implications of earlier cross-Channel flights by Louis Blériot. His flight across the English Channel on 25th July 1909 won him the £1000 prize offered by the London *Daily Mail* for the first successful crossing. Blériot's feat not only advanced the frontiers of aviation – it showed how planes could dramatically extend the reach of any potential invader.

When the 1914-18 war finally broke, aircraft were used only supportively, as the cavalry had once been used, to scout out enemy positions and troop movements. A camaraderie developed between pilots on opposing sides which, for a while, transcended the

The airplane's military role was quickly realized and when World War I broke out in 1914 aircraft design advanced rapidly. Aerial warfare, particularly dog-fights (right), tested pilots and machines to the limit. Many young, promising pilots were killed and surviving was such a matter of luck that those who did lived recklessly after the war. Some found an outlet in air-racing (left), others in pioneering air-routes, or daredevil aerial acrobatics – like the famous stunt flyer Lillian Boyer (below left).

The great adventurers

Not surprisingly, many pilots who survived the War were reluctant to return to humdrum, peacetime routine. Consequently, they looked to other ways of using their new, powerful machines to provide excitement.

Some turned to stunt flying at the aerial circuses which were a craze in post-War America, and which gave them much the same status as daring trapeze artists. Some resumed the thrill and danger of air racing which had begun on an international scale in France in 1911. These races included seaplane trials which reached their climax in the contests for the famous Schneider Trophy. These pushed both man and machine to the limits of human and technological endurance. In 1931, having won the race for the third successive time, Britain earned the right to keep the trophy for ever. The winning plane was a predecessor of the World War II Spitfire.

Other ex-wartime pilots pioneered the early airmail routes, working for the new airlines that sprang up in Germany, Holland and Britain after 1919. Air routes were opened up earliest in under-developed areas, such as French Guyana and Equatorial Africa, where air travel was all the more desirable because rail and road communications were poor or non-existent. The inaccessible Andes in Peru were first flown east-west by an Argentinian army pilot, Teniente Luis de Candelaria, in 1918,

The first all-metal aircraft was the experimental 'Tin Donkey' of 1918. Before this airframes were made of wood, canvas and wire. The first all-metal passenger craft was the Junkers F13 monoplane (below). This development showed the shape of things to come by allowing aircraft to be made stronger, bigger and more powerful.

followed by a west-east flight by a Chilean army pilot eight months later.

By the early 1920s, Britain had four passenger airlines, France had five and Germany had a national company (Lufthansa) and several smaller air transport firms. International routes were flown as early as 1919: London to Paris, Toulouse-Barcelona-Tangier, Paris to Brussels, Florida to Havana, Cuba.

Much longer-distance flights became the preserve of airmen and airwomen with a taste for confronting the unknown. Distance was the one dimension of flying not fully explored during the War. Long-haul ventures began within a few months of the end of the War, spurred on by the various prizes offered by newspapers amidst mounting enthusiasm from a public eager for a taste of these great adventures. Summer 1919 saw three attempts at flying the Atlantic, the first of which ended in partial success when one of three United States Navy flying boats succeeeded in reaching the Azores from Long Island. The other two were forced down into the sea. A British attempt to reach Europe from Newfoundland failed in the same month, but glory was salvaged within weeks by Captain John Alcock and Lieutenant Arthur Whitten Brown, both former wartime pilots, who flew their two-engined Vickers Vimy biplane fitted with long-range tanks, from St. John's, Newfoundland to Clifden, County Galway, Ireland

Geoffrey de Havilland designed World War I fighter planes as well as many of the earliest airliners and gave his name to one of the greatest aircraft manufacturing companies. The De Havilland 34, (above) carried 10 passengers in comfort in the early 1920s.

Amy Johnson (left) became a household name when, in the 1930s, she broke distance records and flew solo England to Australia. She was killed, possibly shot down, in World War II.

Charles Lindbergh (right) achieved a double first when he flew his Ryan monoplane Spirit of St Louis from New York to Paris in May 1927. It was not only the first non-stop solo Atlantic crossing, but the first to link major cities on either side of the ocean. He won $25,000 dollars and the worship of the public.
Lindbergh, accompanied by his wife, went on to survey the Pacific and South Atlantic for prospective scheduled airline routes.

on 14th and 15th June.

The achievement of Alcock and Brown was only one in a rapid succession of endurance flights, most of which had to be made in a series of short hauls. Egypt to India was flown in six hops, in late 1918. Australia was reached from Britain a year later when Ross and Keith Smith flew the 11,294 miles in just under four weeks, also in a Vickers Vimy bomber. The first Britain–South-Africa flight was made in February-March 1920. The first coast-to-coast crossing of the United States in a single day was made by Lieutenant J. H. Doolittle, holder of many height and distance records, in 1922, and the first non-stop crossing by Kelly and Macready in 1923.

Long-distance flights were a gruelling challenge demanding hour upon hour of concentration, and formidable achievements. None more so, perhaps, than Captain Charles Lindbergh's solo crossing of the Atlantic from New York to Paris in his windowless *Spirit of St Louis.* Flying by periscope he was airborne continuously for just over 33½ hours.

Sadly the year of Lindbergh's success, 1927, was notorious for its toll of disasters. Between March and September, 20 aviators disappeared attempting to fly the Atlantic, several of them on the more treacherous east-west route. One of the pilots swallowed by the sea was the eccentric French aviator Charles Nungesser whose aircraft, White Bird, took off from Paris bound for New York so loaded down with fuel that it could barely reach 300 feet.

Read all about it

The development of cinema and radio, and the mass circulation of newspapers ensured universal interest in the conquest of the skies. Charles Lindbergh, mobbed by excited Parisians at Le Bourget airfield, was among the earliest of a new breed of popular hero. Flyers became the focus of world-wide attention. Where disaster or disappearance sealed the fate of a long-distance aviator, he became a legendary figure.

One such was Charles Kingsford-Smith who flew around Australia in 10 days, in 1927, captained the first trans-Pacific flight in 1928, made the first air crossing of the Tasman Sea three months later, crossed the Atlantic in 1930, flew from Australia to the United States in 1934 – then vanished near Singapore while attempting a flight from London to Australia. Amelia Earhart, the American pioneer, captured the public imagination with her solo crossing of the north Atlantic in 1932 and solo flight from Hawaii to California in 1935 – but she disappeared over the South Pacific during an attempt to fly round the world in 1937. Amelia's British counterpart, Amy Johnson, who flew solo London to Australia in 1930 and broke records flying to India, Japan, Capetown and the United States, became a popular heroine, lauded in song:

Amy! Wonderful Amy!
Can you blame me for loving you?
Since you've won the praise of every nation

You have filled my heart with admiration!
Amy! Wonderful Amy!
I'm proud of the way you flew!
Believe me, Amy,
You can't blame me, Amy,
For falling in love with you.

The one-eyed American stunt pilot, Wiley Post, twice flew round the world, in 1931 and 1933. 1933 also saw the first over-flying of Mount Everest, by a British team headed by the Marquess of Clydesdale.

More than just a stunt, the flight enabled part of the Himalayas to be mapped in detail for the first time.

These heroic exploits furthered the developments of aircraft and flying in several ways. Most evident was the simple proof that vast distance, weather, terrain, human frailty and technological stress were no longer insuperable obstacles. The flights mapped out the framework of future passenger air routes and field-tested various pieces of equipment. For instance, Wiley Post's second round-the-world flight showed the value of navigational instruments and

TWOPENCE   EVERY WEDNESDAY

Modern Wonder

Vol. 2. No. 46. Week ending April 2, 1938

"I FLEW at 400 miles an hour — and I thought I was dying..."
A remarkable story inside

GREAT NEW
PRESENTATION
TO EVERY READER

The quest for greater and greater speed captured the public imagination, as records tumbled with every new engine modification. Until 1938 it was believed that the maximum speed possible in a piston-engined airplane was about 400 mph (644 km/h). When the 'magic' 400mph barrier fell in 1938, such speeds were greeted with astonishment – the very stuff of adventure stories (left).

As early as 1928, the Englishman Frank Whittle believed that airplanes could be powered by jet engines: he even convinced the Air Ministry. But the time and money needed for development thwarted Whittle for almost 10 years. As a result the first jet to fly was a German craft, the Heinkel He178, in 1939. The first British jet flew in May 1941. It was another 11 years before commercial airliners were jet powered. Frank Whittle (pictured right, in 1959), was perhaps the last 'hero' of aviation. Aircraft development is no longer left to individuals.

the automatic pilot. The Everest flight of 1933 tested the new supercharged aero-engine and indicated the protection necessary for pilots flying in the freezing temperatures found at heights of 34,000 feet and more. Transatlantic flights led to refinements in aeroplane dynamics, retractable landing gear, cowled engines and to increased speed and reduced fuel consumption. Gradually, through trial, error and refinement, the wood, fabric and wire of early aircraft gave way to all-metal structures – the German Junkers F13 was the first in commercial service – the biplane to the more streamlined and faster monoplane. With metal airframes came bigger, stronger aircraft better able to withstand the stresses and strains imposed by more powerful engines. With increased size came more space, and, therefore, better passenger and freight carrying capacity. And as capacity increased, costs (relatively speaking), fell until air travel came within the reach of many more people.

Towards the jet age

By 1930 the theoretical absolute speed limit for propellor-engined airplanes was calculated to be about 400 mph. And although around this time the fastest speed achieved was only about 300 mph, a few design engineers began to look for alternatives to the propellor engine (the 400 mph barrier was, in fact, not broken until 1938).

In 1930 the Englishman Frank Whittle took out patents on the first jet engine. Similar patents were also lodged by two German jet engine pioneers a

little later, in 1935. However, despite Whittle's five-year lead the jet-engined aircraft was first developed in Germany and, in 1939, the Heinkel HE178 made the world's first jet-powered flight. Quite suddenly, astounding speeds were possible, as demonstrated in the last years of World War 2 when German Messerschmitt Me-262 jets entered the air war in Europe and flew in combat at a then-astonishing 540 mph. The Me-262 and its British counterpart the Gloster Meteor came too late to affect the course of the war but their arrival marked a clear pointer to the future.

Rocket propulsion was also developed in Germany during the War and the V2 rocket developments laid the foundations for space exploration in the late 1950s and 1960s.

The jet engine was used to power passenger liners, the planes themselves becoming larger and larger as more and more people thought in terms of crossing oceans and continents at high speed. Speeds kept on increasing until even supersonic flight – first achieved when an American rocket plane, the Bell X-1, broke the sound barrier in 1947 – was available to the fare-paying passenger. Concorde, developed by Franco-British cooperation, went into service as the first supersonic passenger air-liner in 1974. Now even the ultimate aerial adventure, space travel – first achieved in 1961 – has become commonplace, with the renewal of the Space Shuttle program.

After the Wright Brothers, less than 60 years elapsed between Man first conquering the air and escaping gravity's grasp altogether.

THE GREAT COMPOSERS

George Gershwin

1898–1937

George Gershwin was one of America's finest songwriters, and at the age of 21 he had not only completed his first Broadway score, but had also written a huge hit song, Swanee, which sold millions of copies. During the 1920s, his musical comedies contained several wonderful tunes of enduring popularity. Yet Gershwin also yearned to write for the concert hall. In 1924, he premièred his Rhapsody in Blue, a melodic masterpiece in which Gershwin combined a taste of jazz music with elements of the Romantic tradition. The work, perhaps the best-known orchestral piece written by an American, is analysed with his Concerto in F and I Got Rhythm Variations in the Listener's Guide. *Gershwin's young and spirited music seemed to epitomize the emergence of American popular arts;* In The Background *describes the birth of sound in motion pictures and the development of jazz.*

George Gershwin's journey from New York's Lower East Side to the Upper East Side exemplifies the American dream. Born of Russian immigrant parents, he developed his natural musical abilities as a pianist and song-plugger in Tin Pan Alley. He began to write songs for Broadway; his older brother Ira often contributed lyrics. After an astounding hit with the song Swanee in 1919, he rapidly rose to the top of his profession. His works for the concert hall and his musical comedies were huge successes throughout the 1920s, and a tour of Europe in 1928 confirmed his international reputation. An exuberant, outgoing man, Gershwin seemed to revel in his status as an American hero. Even the relative failure of two Broadway shows and his opera, Porgy and Bess, did not seem to touch him; he moved to Hollywood, enjoying his final triumphs before his death in 1937.

COMPOSER'S LIFE
'I got rhythm'

***From Tin Pan Alley to Carnegie Hall, via Broadway,
George Gershwin's career as composer and
performer of both serious and popular music was
typical of 'rags to riches' stories of American life.***

From 'The Gershwins' by Robert Kimball and Alfred Simon

Bettmann Archive Inc./BBC Hulton Picture Library

The story of George Gershwin's life is almost a stereotype of the typical early 20th century 'rags to riches' story. From his rough-and-ready Lower East Side childhood, he rose, through his music, to become the toast of New York's social set. His music, both the songs he wrote for Broadway and the more serious concert works, brought him fame and wealth.

Gershwin's parents, Rosa and Moishe Gershovitz migrated from St Petersburg in Russia to New York in 1891 and the family name was Americanized as Gershvin and later adapted to Gershwin. Their first son Israel (Ira) was born in 1896 and George, their second son, was born on 26th September 1898.

Ira, George's older brother, was the family scholar and in 1910 his mother purchased a piano for him, but it was George who quickly took to it, playing popular melodies on it. Unknown to the rest of the family, George had become interested in music after hearing a school friend, Maxie Rosenzweig (Max Rosen) play the viola in a school recital. George had been standing outside the school hall; was over-whelmed by the sound and made inquiries until he established who the player was. Then he arranged to meet Maxie. They became firm friends, their shared interest in music being the bond between them.

George's exceptional natural ability on the piano was soon recognized and his parents arranged for him to have lessons. After suffering at the hands of several bad teachers he became a pupil, in 1912, of a particularly able musician and gifted teacher. Charles Hambitzer. Hambitzer realized that George had a great talent and set about organizing his musical knowledge.

Inspired by his teacher's orderly and enthusiastic approach to both old and modern classics, George for a time entertained notions of becoming a concert pianist. Given his lack of interest in academic prowess his parents made a last ditch attempt to give him a stable career and arranged for him to go to an

Born in 1898 George Gershwin (left, shown with, from left to right, his younger brother Arthur, the maid, his mother and older brother, Ira), grew up in the seedy Lower East Side of New York City (above).

accountancy school. However, in 1914 the fifteen-year-old Gershwin persuaded his mother to allow him to leave school to take a job as a song salesman or plugger, promoting the popular song music of the Tin Pan Alley song publisher, Remick's. Tin Pan Alley – its name is thought to derive from the 'tinny' sound of pianos – was the Mecca for popular music. For Gershwin it was an important stepping stone, as it put him in close touch with popular music.

A novice in Tin Pan Alley

His starting salary at Remick's was $15 a week. The job was arduous, had long hours and consisted mostly of playing the piano in a little booth, either accompanying amateur singers or demonstrating the latest Remick songs to parlour pianists. One positive aspect of the job was that it developed his dexterity and stylistic scope. He was successful and was soon in demand with regular clients. Remick's asked him to record some piano rolls for them at $5 a roll, something which he did for them and other publishers for a number of years, to supplement his income.

His ambition, at this stage, was to have some of his own songs published. Remick's were not interested in their top song plugger being a songwriter as well. Not deterred, Gershwin hawked his songs from this period round Tin Pan Alley and by 1917 had a few songs published. Then, too, Remick's decided to publish one of his songs, a Gershwin/Will Donaldson ragtime piano piece, *Rialto Ripples*.

Soon after this George decided on a career on Broadway. He later wrote that 'The popular-song racket began to get definitely on my nerves. Its tunes somehow began to offend me . . . Jerome Kern was

the first composer who made me conscious that most popular music was of inferior quality and that musical-comedy was made of better material.'

The lure of Broadway

Given this attitude, it was no surprise when he left Remick's in March 1917 to make his way into the musical comedy world. He soon found work as an accompanist on small shows, all of which proved to be financial disasters for their producers. This didn't seem to matter to George – he used the shows as a means to meet the right people and to put himself about to the best of his ability. His outgoing, confident personality, coupled with his talent for improvisation on the piano made him a popular man on the productions he worked on.

Word soon got around Broadway that here was someone to be watched. Gershwin came to the attention of Max Dreyfus, the head of Harms publishing house. Dreyfus, an astute man, had a gift of recognizing song-writing talent, and he saw the potential in George Gershwin. In February 1918 Dreyfus signed him to a deal where he was paid $35 per week just to write songs. The immediate result of this was George's first collaboration with his brother Ira in the song *The Real American Folk Song*. It was premièred in a show in 1918 but only published 40 years later when it was recorded by Ella Fitzgerald.

Meanwhile George kept up his work for various productions and occasionally his songs were accepted for inclusion in musicals. He realized that only the composer credited with the music for whole shows made any money on Broadway.

In 1919 he had two important firsts: his first complete Broadway score and his first big song hit. The show was the moderately successful *La La Lucille,* which was also the first production for Alex Aarons, the producer of so many later Gershwin smash successes. The hit song was *Swanee.* Hardly a typical Gershwin tune, it was thrown together by Gershwin and lyricist Irving Caesar in an attempt to cash in on the popularity of a piece of music called *Hindustan.* The song was a flop when it first appeared on Broadway in the show *Capitol Review,* but it was later picked up by Al Jolson who heard Gershwin playing it at a party. Jolson put it into his current show, *Sinbad,* and it quickly became a sensation. With this song, which was to be the single biggest hit of his career, Gershwin had arrived. Al Jolson recorded the song in 1920, sold millions of discs, and boosted the sales of the sheet music tremendously.

Still only 22, Gershwin was a tall, well-developed man. Although not handsome – he had a broken nose, a receding hairline and a thrusting jaw – he seemed to ooze sex appeal. His reputation as a ladies' man grew as he moved into wider and higher circles of New York, Broadway and Hollywood. Conquests came easily to him as he became the darling of the social set. He was always to be seen with a different female companion, and it was common knowledge that as well as having many affairs he was also a

The Kobal Collection

By permission of the British Library

The annual Ziegfeld Follies (publicity material for the 1936 MGM film,* The Great Ziegfeld, *left) started in 1907 was the brainchild of impresario Florenz Ziegfeld. These revues celebrated American femininity in a programme of song and dance both spectacular and extravagant. In 1919 a dancer, George White, formed a rival to the Follies, and from 1920 for four years George Gershwin wrote songs for George White's Scandals (above).

frequent visitor to brothels. Although he had no difficulty in having casual sexual encounters he was never successful in finding a deep romantic attachment of a permanent nature. Despite his reputation Gershwin had many friends both male and female with whom he had companionable relationships. Outwardly a buoyant and exuberant man, his close friends knew that there were times of anxiety and depression, when he worried about his work and career. He developed a physical problem, which he described as 'composer's stomach'. As a result he became obsessed with his diet and resorted to all sorts of food fads to try to cure himself.

Gershwin's career after his hit with *Swanee* was one of increasingly rapid strides to the top of his profession. He was commissioned in 1920 to write the score for the second annual appearance of *George White's Scandals* show – the rival to the spectacular *Ziegfeld Follies* – the musical revues with which Florenz Ziegfeld had wowed Broadway. Gershwin was to write the score for another four of these shows.

During the years he was involved with George White's Scandals Gershwin still kept his hand in with many other Broadway productions. In 1923 he travelled to England for the first time to give his first revue there, *The Rainbow*. It was hardly a triumph but he fell in love with London Society and it with him.

Into the concert hall

By now he had established himself as an experienced show professional but since *Swanee* he had not had any major successes on Broadway. He now had his sights set further afield, not only in theatre but in the concert hall. Here in November 1923 he had a spectacular success, when he accompanied the Canadian soprano, Eva Gauthier in a programme entitled *'Recital of Ancient and Modern Music for Voice'*. Max Jaffee accompanied her in the classical selections and Gershwin in the Modern American section, where two of the songs featured were his own compositions. This section proved to be the hit of the evening and it marked the entry of jazz into the concert hall, as well as the triumph of Gershwin as composer and performer.

Gershwin's attempts to combine jazz and the popular song, and popular music with the concert hall were consolidated in 1924 by the overwhelming success of a work written as a concert piece in the jazz style, *Rhapsody in Blue*. So great was its success that it was obvious to all that Gershwin had arrived not only as a performer, but also as a serious composer. The momentum generated from the triumph of *Rhapsody in Blue* spilled over into Gershwin's next project – the score for his next Broadway hit, starring Fred and Adele Astaire, *Lady, Be Good!* This show, when it opened in November, was a tremendous hit, and had some of Gershwin's most memorable songs. It was also the first show written solely by George and his brother, Ira Gershwin. They had collaborated before but Ira, a more retiring personality than George used a pseudonym. He had not wished to be making his way in show business on his brother's bandwagon. As a bonus to his triumph, earlier in the year, George's second visit to London, for the show *Primrose*, was also a runaway success.

In 1925 Gershwin repeated his triumphs of the previous year with the *Concerto in F*. On Broadway his hit for the year was *Tip-Toes*, again written with Ira. From then until the great commercial and financial upheavals of the Depression, which began in Sep-

Paul Whiteman (shown above, with his orchestra) commissioned George to write a jazz symphony for a concert held at the Aeolian Hall, New York, on 22 February 1924. The work, Rhapsody in Blue, was a great success. Later that year George's concert-hall triumph was further consolidated with the Broadway show, Lady, Be Good! The show marked the first appearance of the brother and sister partnership of Fred and Adele Astaire (right) in a Gershwin musical. The show was significant, too, as the first major Broadway hit for both George and his older brother, the lyricist, Ira Gershwin (far right). They had found the perfect working partnership to produce the glittering musical comedies much in demand on the stages of Broadway (centre). The brothers, opposites in personality (George was bouncy and gregarious, while Ira was quiet and retiring) worked together until George's death in 1937. Ira continued in showbusiness, writing for stage and screen until 1954.

tember 1929 Gershwin went from strength to strength. *Oh, Kay!* in 1926, *Funny Face* in 1927 and *Rosalie* in 1928 were all hugely successful. In 1928 he moved from the large house on 103rd Street which he had bought some years previously for his family to very swish bachelor apartments at 33 Riverside Drive. From childhood he had often sketched and drawn caricatures but in 1927 he became interested in water colour painting. He proved to have a natural talent, and received much help and encouragement from his cousin and friend Henry Botkin. Botkin also assisted him in amassing a very impressive collection of modern masters.

Success abroad

A trip to Europe in 1928 confirmed his international stature – he was lauded and fêted in London, Paris and even in Vienna, where he met and became friendly with the composer Alban Berg. While he was in Paris Gershwin sketched out his next orchestral composition, a tone poem for orchestra, *An American in Paris*. Later that year it was orchestrated and it was premièred at Carnegie Hall on December 13 1928. At a party after the performance Gershwin was honoured by friends who acknowledged him as a leader of young America in music.

The Depression, when it did break, had little material effect on Gershwin's life or career. By this time he was a national hero, his finances were on a firm footing and the hits kept coming. Hollywood was the next goal on the horizon and in 1930 George and Ira made their Hollywood début. They spent four luxurious months writing the music for a determinedly second-rate feature film, *Delicious*. For this they were paid $100,000 and George, in addition, collected $50,000 for giving his permission to use *Rhapsody in Blue* in *The Paul Whiteman Story*. In Hollywood, when he was not actually composing, George spent his time golfing, partying and having flings with starlets. On his return to New York, he wrote the *Second Rhapsody for Orchestra with Piano*. After delays due to the hope that Toscanini might première the work, it was given its first performance in 1932 by Koussevitzky and the Boston Symphony Orchestra, with Gershwin playing the piano part. It was another raging success. However, although he had survived the effects of the bad economic climate his luck seemed to change and in 1933 he and Ira were associated with the ill-fated

In 1928 Gershwin made a trip to Europe. While in Paris he sketched out his next orchestral work, An American in Paris. *It was premièred at Carnegie Hall in December 1928. The following year the ballet choreographed by Harriet Hoctor (right) to the music appeared in the Broadway show,* Show Girl. *Despite lavish musical items in the show, including a spot for Duke Ellington and his band, Show Girl was not a box-office success.*

and poorly-backed show, *Pardon My English.* Not even George's golden touch could save it. This failure seemed to make no impression on him, however, for in the same month he moved to a cavernous apartment, considerably more spacious and luxurious than Riverside Drive.

In the autumn of 1933 Gershwin was pulled up short by another Broadway flop. *Let 'Em Eat Cake,* a sequel to *Of Thee I Sing,* despite its superior music, died very quickly. Up to this point only George's enormous prestige had kept his Broadway shows solvent. Broadway, in general, was having a disastrous time in the Depression. The series of box-office disasters, although they may not have altered his financial situation, certainly affected his equilibrium, and may have led to his decision to undergo psychoanalysis with Dr Gregory Zilboorg in 1934.

Still, creatively he had little to worry about. 1934, for example, was the year he began work on the opera he had been wanting to write for years. He and author Edwin DuBose Heyward, the writer of the novel *Porgy,* had long been planning an opera of it. Gershwin and DuBose Heyward started work on the project, with the help of Ira for the lyrics.

George, to get the uninterrupted peace he needed for such a sustained creative effort, spent two months, dispensing with all social comforts, on Folly Island with Ira and Heyward. There was not even a phone on the island. The isolation worked, and George returned to New York in autumn 1934 with a huge slab of the opera drafted out. By January 1935, working steadily, George completed the orchestration of the opera in time for the Boston opening, in September 1935. Ever since that Boston opening and the following New York opening in October, the full-length opera has aroused criticism and controversy. The New York Post reviewer summed up a general reaction by stating that the opera was 'a hybrid, fluctuating constantly between music-drama, musical comedy, and operetta. It contains numerous 'song-hits' . . . Yet they are too 'set' in treatment, too isolated from the pitch of opera for us to accept them

as integral parts of a tragic music-drama.'

Gershwin's reply was to claim *Porgy and Bess* as a folk-opera, written in a new form faithful to the cultural traditions of the folk it portrayed. Be that as it may, Gershwin and Heyward's opera was not destined to be successful on stage until, in 1942, five years after his death, a considerably reworked version was a hit on Broadway. Even though the songs were individually successful and their sheet music sold well, Porgy and Bess was Gershwin's third flop in a row in the theatre.

It was probably his third failure which prompted both George and Ira to look to Hollywood again. On 9 and 10 July 1936, George played two consecutive nights at New York's Lewishon Stadium. It was an all-Gershwin programme; and it was also his last live appearance in his native city.

For a number of years George Gershwin lived in a cavernous penthouse apartment at 33 Riverside Drive, New York. Every room, including the living room (above) was filled with Gershwin's collection of art treasures and stylish furniture.

IT'S **GERSHWIN!** IT'S **GLORIOUS!** IT'S **GREAT!**

SAMUEL GOLDWYN
PRESENTS
THE MOTION PICTURE PRODUCTION

PORGY and BESS

Hailed wherever it has opened!
**ONE OF THE YEAR'S
10 BEST!**

SIDNEY POITIER · DOROTHY DANDRIDGE · SAMMY DAVIS, JR. · PEARL BAILEY

MUSIC BY GEORGE GERSHWIN | LIBRETTO BY DuBOSE HEYWARD | LYRICS BY DuBOSE HEYWARD and IRA GERSHWIN | SCREENPLAY BY N. RICHARD NASH | DIRECTED BY **OTTO PREMINGER**

FOUNDED ON THE PLAY 'PORGY' BY DuBOSE and DOROTHY HEYWARD | ORIGINALLY PRODUCED FOR THE STAGE BY THE THEATRE GUILD | TECHNICOLOR® | DISTRIBUTED BY COLUMBIA PICTURES

Gershwin read Edwin DuBose Heyward's novel Porgy *in 1926, and at once wrote to him, saying that he wanted to compose an opera based on it. It was not until nine years later that Gershwin and Heyward actually collaborated on the opera,* Porgy and Bess, *(a lobby poster for the 1959 film is shown left). The opera opened in Boston on 30 September 1935 and in New York on 10 October. The critics were not whole-heartedly in favour of Gershwin's mixed use of opera and operetta and the show went on the road. After Gershwin's death it was more successful and by the early 1950s had been seen all over the States and Europe, including the Soviet Union.*

Although he had a reputation as a ladies' man Gershwin did make one or two deeper emotional attachments to women. At least two of these more serious relationships, however, were with married women; women who through their circumstances protected him from having to make a commitment to them. Paulette Goddard (left), for instance, at the time when Gershwin met and fell in love with her, was married to Charles Chaplin.

Return to Hollywood

The second Hollywood sojourn was a distinct artistic and financial success for the Gershwin brothers: they wrote scores for two Fred Astaire movies; *Shall We Dance,* and *A Damsel in Distress.* Both were full of the very best in quality music. Not only did George find creative fulfilment in Hollywood but a rake to the end, he also had many affairs. Despite these he did have one or two more serious relationships; one with Simone Simon, the French actress. By early 1937, he and Ira were into their third movie, *Goldwyn Follies,* and George was in love with Paulette Goddard, Charlie Chaplin's wife. He was deeply hurt when she refused to leave Chaplin.

During June 1937, previously noticed but isolated warning signs that all was not well with this usually robust and healthy person became more persistent. He began to experience frequent dizzy spells and headaches. Since his doctors could find no irregularities, he put these down to stress of overwork and continued to live his life as usual and rejected the idea of having a spinal tap to check for a possible brain tumour. However, over the following month his symptoms recurred with greater frequency and intensity until, on 9 July, 1937 after being weak and dazed for days, he fell into a coma.

A spinal tap performed the following day established the presence of a brain tumour, and it was decided that an emergency operation was the only hope. Early on 11 July this took place, and part of the tumour was removed. About five hours later, Gershwin died without regaining consciousness. Two gigantic funeral ceremonies, one in Hollywood and one in New York, on 15 July 1937, demonstrated the loss felt by Americans at his passing.

Concert works

Already an established song-writer on Broadway, George Gershwin used his brilliance as a melodist to bring jazz, the new music of America, to the concert hall. His works were an instant success.

George Gershwin was primarily a song-writer and as a young man, his talents quickly earned him both fame and fortune with a string of Broadway successes. But Gershwin also yearned to write music that was more serious and lasting and which would find him a way into the more high-brow concert halls that were usually reserved for classical recitals. Around the early 1920s, a vigorous popular music had been emerging out of the spirituals, hymns and work songs of the oppressed Negros, based mainly in the South and around New Orleans. This was Jazz and although at first records were made primarily for the Negro market, white musicians were quick to imitate it and to make its infectious rhythms their own. Jazz was therefore being introduced to the world of mass entertainment and even serious musicians began to take an interest.

The famous jazz band leader Paul Whiteman prompted Gershwin to write the *Rhapsody in Blue,* first performed in 1924, because he was keen that jazz music should be made palatable to the white American middle class. The following year, Walter Damrosch, Director of the New York Symphony Society, also seeing the potential of jazz, commissioned Gershwin to write a concerto.

Gershwin composed a number of serious concert works all of which received widespread acclaim but his music has often been criticized for structural defects. Weakness in composition was no doubt the result of Gershwin's lack of formal musical training but this in no way detracts from the vitality of the the melodies themselves, whose effectiveness in sequence, give the work its immediacy and appeal. The fact that Gershwin's concert works are still so regularly played and given serious attention by musicians of note must, in the end, fully endorse their lasting worth.

Concerto in F

The *Concerto* was Gershwin's second large-scale work, coming hard on the heels of the *Rhapsody in Blue* of the previous year, and premièred at the Carnegie Hall on 3rd December 1925. It was commissioned by Walter Damrosch and written in the form of a classical concerto. Gershwin, with his scant musical training, must have been severely tested by a work of this size. He had accepted the commission without thinking of what was involved and some

say that he actually had to go out and buy a book on orchestration to arm himself with information on what a concerto was.

Although a specific performance date was written into the commission, Gershwin did not start work until the summer, and most of August was spent on the *Concerto*. This was a period of mounting success for Gershwin. His shows *Primrose* and *Lady, Be Good!* (his first collaboration with his brother Ira) had been well received on both sides of the Atlantic and he had recently moved with his family into a large house on West 103rd Street, the better to enjoy his extravagent lifestyle.

The work's original title was the *New York Concerto* and its three movements had an overall plan of 1 – Rhythm, 2 – Melody (Blues), 3 – More Rhythm. By the time the short piano score was finished and the piece was ready to be tried out on his two friends, conductor Bill Daly and Damrosch, Gershwin had revised the title simply to *Concerto in F.* With their approval, he set about orchestrating it and since his skill in this direction was limited, he most probably discussed the ideas that he had with people like Daly, before incorporating them into his final draft.

The *Concerto* was completed on 10th November and the next stage was a complete run through at Gershwin's own expense, with a specially hired orchestra, to be conducted by Bill Daly and with himself as the soloist. Gershwin described this trial run as his 'greatest musical thrill' even though he made some cuts and changes to tighten the work up. The score was then ready for rehearsals with the New York Symphony Orchestra in the Carnegie Hall where it was to be premièred.

At first Gershwin had to coax the players into the jazz idiom, to unwind and flow with the music's bouyant drive – a style which was far removed from the concert traditions of the Carnegie Hall – but soon the orchestra began to swing with the music. Walter Damrosch made a speech at the première in which he paid tribute to the composer for giving the classical world of the concert hall a taste of jazz, the new music of America. He said:

Various composers have been walking around jazz like a cat around a plate of soup waiting for it to cool off, so that they could enjoy it without burning their tongues, hitherto accustomed only to the

Gershwin's serious concert works, like the painting below, exude a young and enthusiastic spirit of contemporary city life. This feeling is encapsulated in the lively Charleston rhythms of his famous Concerto in F.

more tepid liquid distilled by cooks from the classical school. Lady Jazz, adorned with her intriguing rhythms, had danced her way around the world . . . But for all her travels and her sweeping popularity, she has encountered no knight who could lift her to a level that would enable her to be received as a respectable member in musical circles. George Gershwin has achieved this miracle.

Programme notes

Although written for piano and orchestra and to a classical formula, the syncopated rhythms and blues notes of the music make obvious the work's jazz derivations. The whole *Concerto* breathes vitality, youth and energy.

First movement – Allegro

In the words of Gershwin, the opening movement of the Concerto 'employs the Charleston rhythm. It is quick and pulsating, representing the young enthusiastic spirit of American life'. The movement begins with a brisk rhythmic motif given out by sledgehammer blows on the kettledrums. This is immediately undone by the sinuous Charleston rhythm of the horns, clarinet and violas, before the principal theme is introduced by the bassoon. The bassoon's theme assumes more and more definition until its energy dominates the music and leads to the piano's first entry with a second theme. Again the strength of the opening bass note and *glissando* (slide) is dissolved by the quiet and indeterminate blues melody that follows marked *piano*:

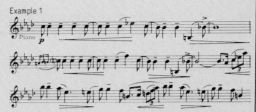

Example 1

but soon the piano is joined by the orchestra as the wistful tune gathers strength. A brief cadenza for the soloist heralds a big orchestral *tutti* as the whole orchestra takes over from the solo instrument with music that could only have come from a Broadway composer. The mood of brimming vitality is briefly restored before this 'three subject' exposition is brought to a close with a

This scene, painted in 1935, of Gershwin in an imaginary concert hall, has a dream-like quality to it, but by 1935, Gershwin's dream of playing before large concert audiences had long become a reality. The première of his first large-scale **work** Rhapsody in Blue *in 1924, followed by the* Concerto in F *in 1925 had brought him instant recognition as a composer and pianist. On both occasions Gershwin was the soloist.*

David Siqueiros 'George in an Imaginary Concert Hall'. From 'The Gershwins' by Robert Kimball and Alfred Simon

majestically scored transformation of the wistful blues melody. A short cadenza then leads into the *development* which elaborates upon what has already been heard but takes as its mainstay the jaunty wide-ranging tune heard first on the bassoon. New material also appears: a fast, syncopated dance and a languorous song-like melody that increases in tension, released in a barbaric Allegro, bitingly rhythmic and under-pinned by the piano's driving persistence *(ostinato)*. Brilliant passage work, a growing sense of urgency and dramatic crescendo all lead to a repeat of the piano's first melody, which is marked *Grandioso* (with grandiloquence) and scored fortissimo for full orchestra. All the time, the piano's pulsating chords push the music forwards to the coda which is really a massively expanded version of the bassoon's opening. After a short virtuoso display by the soloist, the music careers to a breathless close.

Second movement – Andante con moto
A smoky trumpet tune immediately envelops the listener in the heavy languor of a warm city night. Gershwin described this movement as having 'a poetic nocturnal atmosphere which has come to be referred to as the "American blues", but in a purer form than that in which they are usually treated'. The trumpet's quiet, poignant tune seems at first to be trapped by its own inertness but the mood is briskly broken by the piano's entry and a crisp dance tune that injects bustle and life into the music. The piano's strong *oom-cha* rhythm echoes the main subject until the lazy mood of the opening returns with a solo violin gently mulling over what has just been played and the trumpet recommencing its wailing soliloquy. Then a piano cadenza leads into the heart of the movement and one of Gershwin's loveliest broad, song-like melodies that swell passionately in the grandest romantic concerto style:

Example 2

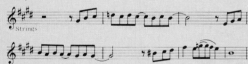

The music grows to a climax and with only a brief backwards glance to the languid music at the movement's opening, it quickly subsides to a close.

Third movement – Allegro agitato
The final movement reverts to the style of the first. 'It is an orgy of rhythms, starting violently and keeping to the same pace throughout', wrote Gershwin. The movement is in a rondo form and the spiky, toccata-like ritornello (the music that returns at certain points during the rondo) is easily recognisable by its driving rhythmic energy and it provides a perfect foil to the more melodic episodes. The first of these is a *marcato* (marked, emphatic)

version of the piano's first melody in the opening movement. After the ritornello, a new, boisterous figure is played on the violins and trumpet, separated by a sequence of quiet chords from a skittish hoe-down dance tune. Then another familiar melody is woven into the texture: this time it is the big tune from the second movement (example 2). There follows some furious contrapuntal writing and more backward and forward references – this time to the piano's entry in the Andante, played here by the violins. The same sequence of big, rising chords heard

Music' by the Canadian soprano, Eva Gauthier and heard Gershwin playing. Whiteman decided to arrange a concert for his own band, and to ask Gershwin, by now one of America's fastest rising young musicians, to write a new jazz work.

Gershwin agreed but, busy as usual, on Broadway projects, the work hardly progressed beyond random jottings made from improvising at the piano. Suddenly however on January 4th 1924, he was spurred into action when he saw a news item in the New York Tribune, reporting that the Whiteman concert would take

Martin Lewis 'The Glow of the City'. Collection, The Museum of Modern Art, New York

in the first movement builds the music to a huge climax, when a single crash of the gong announces a grand overwhelming restatement of the first movement's second subject. The ritornello, hurtling along almost beyond the bounds of safety, brings the concerto to a rousing conclusion.

Rhapsody in Blue

The *Rhapsody in Blue* for jazz band and piano commission preceded the *Concerto* by a little less than a year but it came about for similar reasons – as an attempt to make jazz acceptable in the concert hall. The difference with the *Rhapsody* was however, that the commissioner was himself a jazz musician. Paul Whiteman was one of the first people to exploit jazz seriously. Whiteman was a famous and influential figure who was also a skilled entrepreneur. His idea of taking jazz away from smoky nightclubs and dance halls was boosted when, towards the end of 1923, he attended a 'Recital of Ancient and Modern

The velvet sensuality of a hot city night (above) is the theme expressed in the Concerto in F's second movement. It forms a sharp contrast to the other two movements which are full of the colour and pulsating dance rhythms of the metropolis (right).

place on 12th February and that Gershwin was 'at work on a jazz concerto'.

Gershwin's first plan had been to write an extended jazz blues called *American Rhapsody,* but on the suggestion by his brother Ira, he later changed the title to *Rhapsody in Blue.* The inspiration for the work came to him while he was on a train journey to Boston: He wrote:

And there I suddenly heard – even saw on paper – the complete construction of the rhapsody, from beginning to end ... I heard it as a musical kaleidoscope of America – of our vast melting pot, of our unduplicated national pep, of our blues, our metropolitan madness.'

Understanding music: jazz

Despite jazz's rather 'seedy' background and reputation, the new music quickly won respect as a musical form with many composers of classical music. Indeed, the inventiveness and virtuosity of the early jazzmen influenced and fascinated a generation of composers across the world.

Mighty Stravinsky, for example, succumbed to its influence almost from the outset – even before he had actually heard any jazz: he made its acquaintance through sheet music. His interest later manifested itself in several jazz compositions such as *Piano-Rag-Music, Ragtime for 11 Instruments* and *The Soldier's Tale.* These, inevitably, are much more sophisticated than their simple originals yet retain the verve and vibrancy that is the essence of jazz. Stravinsky's style then moved toward neoclassicism but he returned to symphonic jazz as late as 1945.

Stravinsky spent many years of his life as a French citizen, and the French had always been receptive to American popular music, as shown by Debussy's piano piece *Golliwog's Cakewalk.* The iconoclastic attitude of Satie and 'Les Six' was also well served by the mildly shocking quality of the new black music that began to be heard in the clubs of Paris. The most successful incorporation of jazz into concert music which this group produced is arguably Milhaud's *La Création du Monde,* a ballet score from 1923. The prominence of axophone and trumpet in the 18-piece ensemble, and the use of blues in the melodic writing combine to give this work a unique flavour.

The 'senior' French composers were not immune either: 'Have you been to hear the Negroes?' Ravel wrote to a friend, 'their virtuosity is at times terrifying . . .' His violin onata of 1927 has a central movement called 'Blues' in which the sultry violin blues tune is heard over an implacable 'tick-ock' accompaniment, evoking the long nights the insomniac composer would while away in Parisian night clubs.

Not all the composers working in Paris were French, two other notables were the Russian, Prokofiev, and Bohuslav Martinu 1890-1959), a Czech. The former was little influenced in any profound sense by jazz although hostile critics sometimes thought so: 'Fifteen minutes of Russian jazz with some Bolshevist flourishes,' wrote one of the opera, *The Love of Three Oranges!* Martinu, on the other hand, wrote a series of jazz-inspired pieces in the 1920s which have actually harmed his subsequent reputation. The enjoyable banality of the orchestral *Le Jazz* is too easily taken as typical by those unacquainted with Martinu's later, and superior music.

One of the most successful of all serious works employing jazz was written, however, by the Viennese composer Ernst Krenek b.1900). His opera, *Jonny spielt auf,* with its contemporary setting and jazz idioms, was first performed in 1927 in Leipzig and soon after, in over a hundred other places — such was the impact of the work which tells of a black jazz musician and his involvements with white women. Equally successful initially, but with a more enduring subsequent popularity, was Kurt Weill's *The Threepenny Opera* (1928) to a libretto by Bertolt Brecht based on John Gay's *The Beggar's Opera.* The popular songs in this score actually owe more to German cabaret songs than to American models. There is an irony, therefore, in the appropriation by such real jazz musicians as Louis Armstrong and Ella Fitzgerald of the opening ballad which became *Mack the Knife.*

Many other composers were influenced by jazz between the wars, but in almost all cases though, it was shortlived or shallow — essentially because, as Krenek suggested, great composers found it 'a seasoning, rather than a source of nourishment'.

Jazz swept through the nightclubs of post-war Europe where many a 'serious' composer was seduced by its exhilarating rhythms and unorthodox improvisations.

Otto Dix 'Les Noctambules'. Private Collection. Edimedia

Edward Burra 'Silver Dollar Bar'. Courtesy of the Lefevre Gallery, London

Gershwin began working at great speed and the two-piano short score was ready to be orchestrated only three weeks later. Because of his limited skill in orchestrating and also the lack of time, he left this task to Ferde Grofé, an extraordinarily talented, all round musician and arranger, who also played in Whiteman's band. It is through Grofé's keen ear for instrumental colour and nuance that we know the work today. Since he also knew the capabilities of many of the players, he was able to write, for the first performances at least, with particular people in mind.

With the orchestration completed, there were only five days left for rehearsals. During this time, Whiteman was also involved in promoting the concert, which he called 'Experiment in Modern Music', making sure that critics and influential people in the arts world attended rehearsals. There was a mounting sense of excitement as it was the first major occasion that the vibrant voice of American popular music had launched itself into the arena of 'art' music.

Unfortunately, the concert on the 12th February 1924 at the Aeolian Hall, scarcely lived up to expectations. People were disappointed with most of the 23 items in the programme — consisting only of louder, more fully orchestrated versions of songs that they already knew and, 'in the field of the 'classics', there was nothing more adventurous than Elgar's *Pomp and Circumstance March No. 1* to round the concert off. The audience were getting bored and were beginning to leave when Gershwin took his place at the piano for the penultimate item. His performance turned what could have been a colossal disaster for Whiteman into a huge success and the event put Gershwin on the map as a serious composer. Reception of the work was sensational and it went on to earn for Gershwin and his estate, huge sums of money — a quarter of a million dollars in the ten years following its memorable first performance.

Programme notes

The *Rhapsody in Blue* is a work filled with powerful melody. Gershwin's genius as a melodist has been compared with Tchaikovsky's and indeed, the effectiveness and brilliant inspiration of his themes cannot be questioned. Some people however, have commented upon the weak construction of his music — the conductor Leonard Bernstein described the *Rhapsody* as 'not a composition at all. It's a string of separate paragraphs stuck together – with a thin paste of flour and water'. Gershwin himself knew his weakness in this area but thought that his melodies provided an overall sense of momentum. He was right – despite its faults, the *Rhapsody,* with its irresistible blend of excitement, repose, tension, crescendo and climax, has withstood the test of time and secured a lasting place in the repertoire of classical music.

The first few bars of the *Rhapsody* make one of the most memorable openings to a piece of music.

Ironically, they were not wholly Gershwin's own. He had originally written a rising scale passage for the clarinet, but during rehearsals, the clarinettist Ross Gorman started fooling around with it, exaggerating the length of the notes, and joining them together in a sleazy glissando, with a

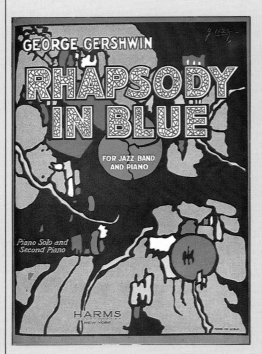

characteristic wail at the top of the run. Gershwin so liked the effect that he kept it in and the change was included in the published score. After the orchestra has introduced its main theme there is a return to the clarinet's run with a downward curling section of the melody, this time on trumpet with *wha-wha* mute, which brings in the piano and a fortissimo restatement of Example 3. Four long candenzas split the work into its main sections and in the first of these, the piano reflects upon what has just been heard as it returns to a vigorous repeat of the main theme. With a mood of mounting excitement, it soon breaks into a new rising

figure, echoed between piano and strings, and a new trumpet tune, scored against a light piano and orchestral accompaniment. The excitement is frozen for a moment by a short solo from the clarinet that seems to have lost its way, before the whole orchestra makes a foot-tapping return to the opening.

Trumpet, clarinet and trombone solos share the short transition to a lively dance tune, which gives prominence to the saxophones. This leads in turn to the second candenza, where once more the soloist ruminates upon what has already been heard and yields to a skittish version of the main blues theme, which is this time rescored for oboes and clarinets with the piano part darting lightly over the keyboard. The third candenza prepares the way for the central slow section, based on a warm love song with characteristic counter melody:

This grows in strength as the music moves through the whole orchestra, but the last candenza arrives and gently breaks the spell as it converts the love song into the lively finale. More virtuoso fireworks for the piano move to a grandiose reprise of the Rhapsody's main theme which is massively scored and brings the work to a triumphant close.

I Got Rhythm Variations

In 1934 Gershwin premièred a new work for piano and orchestra, and it was based on an earlier hit song he had written for the show *Girl Crazy,* produced on Broadway in 1930. The song provided Gershwin with a basis for using his powers of improvisation and ingenuity and it is interesting that though a complex work, much of the Variations was composed away from the piano. Gershwin wrote it during his studies with Joseph Schillinger, a professor who had evolved a system of composing to exact scientific principles, and no doubt these theories had a considerable influence on his orchestration and overall technique.

The *I got rhythm variations* were completed only a matter of days before the start of an extensive concert tour beginning in Boston on 14th January 1934 and which was to take Gershwin together with a fifty-strong orchestra and his conductor Charles Prevain, into forty

The **Rhapsody in Blue** *(original title page, left) is written in the form of a single movement of a concerto. The piece, with its prominent jazz derivations, is a powerful evocation of the 'American Blues'. Edward Hopper expresses a similar mood of bitter-sweet sadness in this beautiful moonlit scene (right).*

Jazz, born out of the black work songs, soon became regarded by white musicians as the new music of America. With its lively syncopated rhythms and blues notes, it provided Gershwin with the perfect idiom for creating musical pictures of his native city (right) and what he called 'America – our vast melting pot'.

Edward Burra 'Harlem'. The Tate Gallery, London. John Webb

cities and over 12,000 miles through the United States and Canada.

Programme notes

Gershwin composed the *Variations* because he had become rather boréd with playing the ever-popular *Rhapsody* and *Concerto,* and he needed a new show-piece. This the work became and, even if it does not have quite the level of inspiration of the earlier works, is a fine example of Gershwin's boundless facility for playing with and teasing the outline of melody.

The *I Got Rhythm* theme is eased into gradually with a solo clarinet playing its first four notes, passing them to the piano and then on to the full orchestra, with the chorus eventually being placed complete. Gershwin describes this first variation as 'simple'. In the second the saxophone has the melody, embellished by highly chromatic writing for the piano, which then takes over with the second half of the theme. The third is a slow waltz with the tune in the orchestra highlighted by the piano's splashing chords and the mood hovering between the grand and the whimsical. The fourth variation is a beautifully orchestrated bit of Chinoiserie where special effects from the xylophone and cymbals are given added spice by some tongue in cheek orientalisms from the piano. The blues dominate the fifth variation where an expressive clarinet solo sets the mood, followed by an equally soulful piano solo. The finale gives the theme the big band treatment and leads to a lively conclusion.

Great interpreters

Edo de Waart (conductor)
De Waart was born in Amsterdam in 1941, and as a boy wanted to be a conductor after seeing Josef Krips in action. He studied at the Amsterdam Music Lyceum, with the oboe as his principal subject, before going on to study conducting. In 1963 still in his early twenties, he joined the Concert-gebouw as first oboist. A year later he took a conducting course at Netherlands Radio and soon made his début as a conductor with the Netherlands Radio Philharmonic Orchestra.

In 1966 he was appointed artistic director and conductor of the Netherlands Wind Ensemble. Later in the year he was also appointed assistant to the conductor Bernard Haitink with the Concertgebouw. This was a giant step for him, and by the late sixties he had conducted over a score of concerts even completing a tour of the U.S.A. with them. In addition, during this period both he and the Wind Ensemble completed a remarkable series of Mozart recordings for Philips.

In 1973 he became artistic director of the Rotterdam Philharmonic, then permanent conductor of the San Francisco

Werner Hass (pianist)

Symphony from 1977-85. In 1986 he was named music director and principal conductor of the Minnesota Orchestra.

Monte Carlo Opera Orchestra
The Orchestra was founded in 1863. Important later conductors included Paul Paray, 1928-44, and Louis Fremaux, 1956-65. Fremaux introduced a series of concerts in the royal palace in Monaco in 1959. Subsequently the orchestra made many recordings with noted soloists like Werner Hass. It also has a fine reputation in opera and ballet productions.

How could it fail? The first 'talkie', a box-office star and a title to whet middle-class appetites: The Jazz Singer! Jazz (though nowhere to be seen in the film) was white America's latest discovery.

104

The nightclub audience applauded rapturously as Al Jolson belted out the final lyric of *Toot, Toot, Tootsie, Goodbye!* As film extras on the set of *The Jazz Singer* they were paid to do so. Not so the New Yorkers who gazed up at the silver screen on the evening of 6 October 1927, watching the film's première. They had paid handsomely to see the fabulous Jolson. But they got their money's worth.

The applause was cut short by Jolson himself. Looking directly into the camera, he broke into speech. In that rasping, strident voice familiar to generations of vaudeville fans, he blurted out, 'Wait a minute! Wait a minute! You ain't heard nothin' yet!' The lucky New York audience, in hearing that, had heard the 'somethin'' they were waiting for – they had just witnessed the birth of the 'talkie', and the greatest transformation in the history of the cinema was suddenly underway.

The sound of the silents
In retrospect, it may seem surprising that talkies took so long to arrive. The cinema was some 30 years old by 1927, and had reached very high technical and artistic standards. Sound reproduction, too, was long past its infancy. The idea of combining sound with film was simple enough in theory: as early as the 1880s, Thomas Edison had tried to harness his recently-invented phonograph machine to the moving pictures of his brand-new Kinetoscope – a peepshow forerunner of cinema. He was balked, however, by the problem of synchronization. He simply could not match sound to the moving pictures with enough precision – and as is known to anyone who has seen sound and pictures go even slightly awry, the results are simply laughable. Others tried and failed, too. So it was that the industry, and Hollywood in particular, matured and flourished within the conventions of silent film.

'Silent' is something of a misnomer. No one ever watched a silent movie in silence. From the beginning, live music accompanied the flickering images on screen. Even the humblest little cinema houses had a piano, while the grand picture palaces in big cities installed massive Wurlitzer organs and even small orchestras. On occasion, distinguished composers were commissioned to write original scores. Saint-Saens, for example, provided one for the celebrated film, *L'Assassinat du Duc de Guise* in 1908.

Sound effects, too, accompanied the action on the

D.W. GRIFFITH'S
· AMERICAN INSTITUTION ·
THE BIRTH OF A NATION
"THE SUPREME PICTURE OF ALL TIME"
NEW YORK MAIL
MAY 2ND 1921

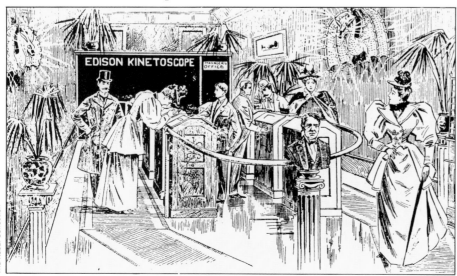

The art of silent cinematography reached levels of outstanding technical proficiency as in the classic The Birth of a Nation *(above). But Hollywood was shrewd enough to see that film-makers had to adapt or, like dinosaurs, become extinct.*

Thomas Edison had achieved rudimentary sound synchronization with his Kinetoscope (an animated peepshow), left, linked to a phonograph by string. He called it the Kinetophone (right).

screen. Horses' hooves clattered, waves crashed against the shore, steam locomotives puffed along the rails. As with music, though, the cinema owner was constrained by the money he could afford on equipment and the skill of those he could employ to work it. There was much variation in quality.

The only way of achieving anything like uniformity of performances was to devize a means of reproducing sound mechanically. By the 1920s the gramophone was no longer the primitive, hand-wound instrument invented by Edison, but a machine essentially similar to the one we know today. The music was both recorded and reproduced electrically. At the same time, the rapid development of radio was giving impetus to the whole field of sound projection. The giant electrical companies were quick to see the implications for the cinema and, by the middle of the 1920s, were urging rival systems of sound reproduction on Hollywood.

Hollywood submits to sound

The vast majority of people involved in film-making would have liked to ward off talkies. They had good reason. Having persuaded an entire generation to accept the conventions of silent film, and having perfected the art, why change? Why tamper with a winning formula, especially when, to do so, would present a host of problems and cost a mint of money.

They had no choice. Radio posed a mortal threat to the cinema, just as television would do to both a generation later. The novelty value of being able to hear a disembodied voice in the comfort of the living room showed no signs of wearing off. The public had acquired a taste for sound. Steeply declining box-office figures proved it. Hollywood would have to adapt or die.

Warner Brothers moved decisively in 1926. Using a synchronized disk system – Vitaphone – developed by Western Electric, they produced the silent classic *Don Juan* with a fully synchronized musical score. The film was warmly received, and Warners were sufficiently encouraged to commit themselves publicly to sound in the future. All they needed was the right vehicle to launch the revolution. They found it in the Broadway smash hit, *The Jazz Singer*.

The Jazz Singer is a sentimental tale about an immigrant cantor's son who forsakes home and synagogue for the bright lights of the theatre. His rebellion, his father's rage and his mother's pleas are finally reconciled as the old cantor lies dying. Then

BBC Hulton Picture Library

It took the threat of radio, and wholesale closure of cinemas, to jolt silent-movie makers out of their complacency. Al Jolson, (left), a huge star of vaudeville, must have been similarly conscious of the threat to his livelihood.

The problems involved in filming with microphones were enormous. At first, the cameras were so noisy that they had to be operated from inside a padded booth (below), eliminating all movement. And since the cameras could not move, neither could the actors.

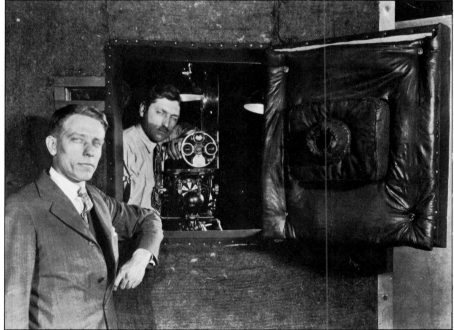

The Kobal Collection

the mother proudly watches her son perform triumphantly on stage. The story is very loosely based on the early career of Al Jolson.

In casting Jolson himself in the title role, Warners guaranteed themselves a box office success. Modestly billing himself as 'the world's greatest entertainer', Jolson was at the peak of one of the most phenomenal careers in the history of show business. A string of hit records had made him a household name across America, among them *Swannee, My Mammy* and *California, here I come*. As a stage performer he was unrivalled: he simply mesmerized his audience. Robert Benchley, a witty and trenchant critic, was left groping for words to describe a Jolson performance he witnessed at New York's Winter Garden in 1925:

When Jolson enters it is as if an electric current had been run along the wires under the seats ... the house comes to tumultuous attention. He speaks,

rolls his eyes, compresses his lips, and it is all over. You are a member of the Al Jolson Association. He trembles his underlip and your heart breaks with a loud snap. He sings a banal song and you totter out to send a night letter to your mother. Such a giving out of vitality, personality, charm and whatever all those words are, results from a Jolson performance.

The Jolson magic

Most of *The Jazz Singer* was shot as a silent film with separate musical accompaniment, but Jolson's songs were recorded synchronously. Since these were songs he had already made famous, they could hardly fail. What sent the audiences into ecstasy, however, were the two occasions when Jolson actually spoke on film. 'You ain't heard nothin' yet!' had been Jolson's catchphrase for 25 years and it brought the house down wherever *The Jazz Singer* played. When, after crooning *My Mammy* on bended knee, Jolson cries out to his mother in the audience, 'Did you like that, Mama?', there wasn't a dry eye in

Stars like Gilbert and Garbo (above) had to speak or die. Greta Garbo had a voice which matched, even enhanced, her image. Her greatest fame was still to come (right). John Gilbert, with his 'Mickey Mouse' voice, plunged to obscurity almost overnight.

cinema houses anywhere.

The overwhelming success of *The Jazz Singer* decided the future of the motion picture industry. Virtually overnight, the silent cinema became obsolete, as all the major studios worked frantically to re-equip. During 1928 about 80 feature films were made with at least some kind of sound component. But the transition was every bit as fraught as the film industry had feared. It was hideously expensive. MGM practically rebuilt their huge studios — complete with a huge *Quiet Please* notice painted on the roof of the (supposedly) sound-proofed studio in the hope of discouraging aircraft. Universal Studios laid out two million dollars on conversion, and it was estimated that Hollywood as a whole, by the middle

Metro-Goldwyn-Mayer PRÉSENTE

GRETA GARBO · RO TAY

dans

Le roman de Margueri

avec LIONEL BARRYMORE

ELIZABETH ALLAN · JESSIE RALPH · HENRY DANIELL · LENORE ULRIC

Réalisation de GEORGE CUKOR

IMPRIMÉ EN FRANCE

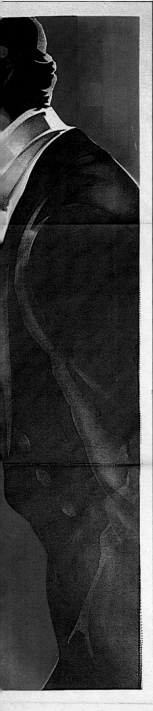

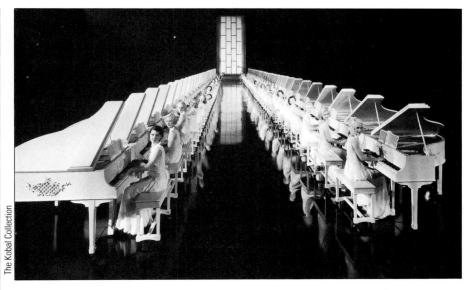

One of the all-time box-office hits, Singin' in the Rain (bottom), could afford to look back at the genesis of sound – the elaborate sound-rigging, the humiliation of silent-screen-goddesses – and laugh. Cinema had survived to see a new golden era, dazzling with the musical spectaculars of Busby Berkeley (left), the epics of Cecil B. de Mille (below left), and a galaxy of stars.

of 1929, had spent about $50 million.

Inside the new studios, cutting out unwanted sound was a nightmare. The Vitaphone microphones were sensitive enough to pick up the whirring of the cameras and the hiss of the arc lights. Camera and camera operator had to be shut up in a tiny, sound-insulated cabin, with the lens poking out of a sound-proofed tube. This was not only a gross inconvenience for the cameraman; it badly restricted the scope of his craft.

Directors, too, had problems. On silent-film sets they could direct the actors while the cameras were running. Although most adapted to the need for silence, there were attempts to continue with the older methods: when Lionel Barrymore was directing *Madame X* in 1929, he attached fine wires to his stars' bodies so that he could, by small electric shocks, signal to them during filming.

Silent film sets had been bedlam – directors bellowing instructions, propmen hauling scenery about, carpenters hammering, bit players chattering off-camera. All that had to end. 'Quiet! Quiet!' became the command repeated endlessly, the echo fading away into an eerie total silence. The actors found this silence almost unendurable – director Frank Capra recalls that many of them could not stop shaking as they faced the camera's unblinking eye amid tomb-like stillness.

Equipment was such that the actor was obliged to address the microphone directly, at close quarters. So the microphone had to be concealed in a strategic

place for every scene. It might be taped to the back of an actor who then stood rooted to the spot for the entire scene, or it might be stuck in a flower vase, forcing the actors into inexplicably strange movements and positions. The results were often unintentionally comic.

But these purely technical difficulties were quickly overcome. The camera cabin could be fitted on wheels or castors. Then camera mobility was restored completely by the development of soundproof camera casing. Fixed microphones gave way to the boom – a pole with the microphone at one end, which could be moved around, out-of-camera, above the actors' heads.

The human factor

The biggest challenge for the actors, however, was not so simply met; for many it meant the swift and inglorious end to a glittering career. For those who had no live-stage experience, it could be the first time in their professional lives that they had had to *speak*.

Today, the skill of delivering dialogue effectively is so much a part of our notion of acting that it is difficult to imagine the collective shudder that ran through the Hollywood acting fraternity at the prospect of it. That classic film, *Singin' in the Rain* affectionately parodies the crisis that confronted the

luscious-looking but vinegar-voiced stars.

Courses in elocution were the rage, while some of the more prudent stars took a brief respite from films to work in repertory theatres and vaudeville to polish their vocal skills. For many, the transition proved impossible. John Gilbert was probably the most notable casualty. Gilbert, a silent-screen superstar, was idolized by millions of women and envied by as many men for his good-looks. But his voice slightly resembled Mickey Mouse's, and his career faded quickly. The dilemma of those such as Gilbert was neatly expressed in a little rhyme of the time:

I cannot talk – I cannot sing
Nor screech nor moan nor anything.
Possessing all these fatal strictures,
What chance have I in motion pictures?

Stars rising

Some of the greatest silent stars took the sound revolution in their stride, however. Greta Garbo managed it with ease, turning her heavy Swedish accent to her advantage. Laurel and Hardy found that it suited their comic gifts perfectly. And even the greatest exponent of silent cinematography, Charlie Chaplin, succeeded with sound when he finally came to accept that he must do so or give up film-making.

To swell the ranks of Hollywood actors who could handle speech, came a host of talented stage actors from New York's Broadway and from Britain. Their arrival coincided with the technical improvements that made possible realistic screen drama and which ushered in Hollywood's second golden age. In the 1930s came the stars: James Cagney, Edward G. Robinson, Clark Gable, Charles Laughton, and a whole galaxy more whose films continue to thrive thanks to television.

The sound cinema, ushered in by Al Jolson's 'You ain't heard nothin' yet!' had reached maturity with

Popperfoto

Bettmann Archive Inc./BBC Hulton Picture Library

Folk jazz found a new form in New Orleans where, for the first time, it was orchestrated for professional bands, in such unsalubrious surroundings as Canal Street (above). Such places are now revered as the cradles of jazz and immortalized in the music 'written' there: Canal Street Blues, *for instance.*

Ragtime syncopation brought a complexity and irresistible bounce to jazz melodies that won a great many converts. Its finest exponent was the blind pianist/composer, Scott Joplin (left) whose work had the quality to endure.

King Oliver's Jazz Band (right), was one of the first to hit the 'big time'. All its members were virtuoso musicians, none more so than (Daniel) Louis Armstrong (centre, on trumpet). His story was typical: a self-taught orphan waif from New Orleans who rose to fame in a society which, 10 years before, would not have spared him a dime.

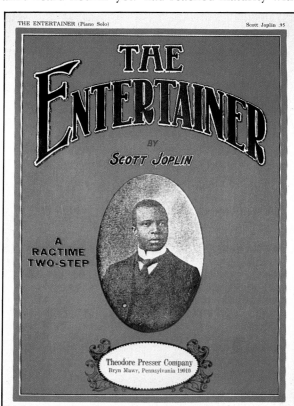

Courtesy of Library and Museum of the Performing Arts, Lincoln Center

astonishing speed – outpacing even D. W. Griffith's bold prediction: Griffith, perhaps the greatest of silent film directors, gave a warmer welcome to sound than many of his peers:

Talkies, squeakies, moanies, songies, squawkies . . . just give them 10 years to develop and you're going to see the greatest artistic medium the world has known.

Jazz without Jolson
For all its significance in the history of the cinema, *The Jazz Singer* had no significance at all to jazz-lovers. The blacked face that was Jolson's trademark was, at best, an unconscious insult to the cultural tradition from which jazz came. To white, middle-class Americans, the word 'jazz' was risqué, loaded with sexual and (worse still) *black* connotations. But those who disliked jazz and all it stood for – 'booze, brothels and blues' was a familiar jibe – were ignoring a vibrant, new musical form.

The roots of jazz
The origins of jazz lie in African percussive rhythms. Work songs and chants from the cottonfields, spirituals and blues gradually fused with European melodies, particularly folksong. Blues songs combined spontaneous improvization with a fixed, three-line form.

The greatest exponent of the blues was W. G. Handy (1873-1958). He was both an archivist, preserving and publishing anthologies of blues and spirituals, and a composer. Handy's works include *Memphis Blues* and *St Louis Blues.*

Ragtime and Dixie
Another important influence on the development of jazz was ragtime, brought to a high level of excellence by the brilliant composer and pianist, Scott Joplin (1868-1917). Joplin's intricate compositions have combined melody with an infectious rhythm based on syncopation.

Ironically, neither Handy nor Joplin was from New Orleans, traditionally considered the home of jazz. The New Orleans style was the original orchestral jazz, and its first great exponents were the members of the Dixieland Jazz Band of 1917. The rollicking Dixieland sound provided background music in the notorious 'red-light' district of Storyville. When Storyville was closed down by the US Navy in 1918, jazz began to move north.

Big city jazz
The exodus from Storyville at the end of World War I had a crucial effect on jazz. Jazz bands established themselves along the Mississippi River in Memphis, St Louis, Louisville and beyond. Other jazz musicians moved farther north still, to Detroit, to New York's Harlem district and to Chicago.

In the early 1920s Chicago established itself as the headquarters of jazz. King Oliver's Creole Jazz Band was at the top of the tree, with the young Louis Armstrong playing second trumpet to the great 'King' himself. A little later, Armstrong displayed the full range of his virtuosity with his own groups, the Hot Five and the Hot Seven. 'Jelly Roll' Morton and his Red Hot Peppers were there at the same time.

By 1930 the rough edges were being smoothed off jazz, something lamented by jazz purists. There are several possible reasons. Many of the great originals wore themselves out with hard living, a phenomenon repeated by a later generation of pop musicians. Secondly, the tendency towards bigger and bigger bands had the effect of sweetening music – making it better for dancing to, but robbing it of much of its vitality. This trend coincided with a change in public taste, and jazz became caught up in that change. As the music became less raucous, more refined, it became more respectable, too. Whatever their original reaction to jazz, many whites had come to accept and enjoy jazz rhythms.

This is not to say that jazz music of the 1930s was utterly harmless. Though dominated by white tastes, it still possessed great black performers and composers in the vanguard of the new, 'sophisticated' jazz – in particular the supremely gifted Duke Ellington. White musicians of great originality were also now working within the idiom. The splendid cornetist, 'Bix' Biederbecke had already demonstrated that to be white was no bar to jazz brilliance, as the clarinetist Benny Goodman and a host of others would later prove. Popular composers like Irving Berlin and Jerome Kern found in jazz a rich mine for their melodic invention, while George Gershwin aspired to greater heights. He not only took jazz seriously, as a legitimate form of American folk music, but he set himself the task of making it the basis of serious symphonic works of lasting value. The result was *Rhapsody in Blue.*

Contemporary composers

Irving Berlin (1888-1989)

Irving Berlin was perhaps the most prolific and successful composer that Tin Pan Alley ever produced. He was born in Russia and emigrated to New York with his family when he was four. He worked as a newspaper vendor and a singing waiter, and in 1911 wrote his first hit song, *Alexander's Ragtime Band*. Over the next twenty years he wrote many successful songs for Broadway revues and in the 1930s he scored equal triumphs in Hollywood. He returned to New York and continued to write for the musical theatre. His most famous songs include *God Bless America, Easter Parade* and *White Christmas*.

Jerome Kern (1885-1945)

The music of Jerome Kern helped to establish the age of American dominance in the musical theatre. He began his career as a song-plugger in New York and quickly became famous for his sophisticated musical comedies. Kern was one of the first composers to integrate his songs into the plot of the musical; he used this technique to great effect in his biggest Broadway success, *Showboat* (1927). He contributed scores to a number of Hollywood films, including *Swing Time* (1936) and *Cover Girl* (1944). Perhaps his most famous song is *Smoke Gets in Your Eyes*.

Zoltán Kodály (1882-1967)

Kodály began to compose in his childhood in Kecskemét, Hungary. After completing his doctoral thesis at Budapest University on Hungarian folk music, he and Bartók travelled throughout Hungary, compiling and collecting folk songs. Like Bartók, he used folk elements in his works, which included the opera *Háry János* (1926) and the choral work *Psalmus hungaricus* (1923). He became interested in music education after working with a boys' choir, developing a school music curriculum and writing music for students. He continued to compose in Budapest until his death in 1967.

Erik Satie (1866-1925)

A leader in the development of modern music, Satie was born in Honfleur, France. He studied at the Paris Conservatoire, then supported himself as a cafe pianist in Montmartre before beginning to compose in earnest. His piano works are characterized not only by their childlike simplicity, but also by their bizzare titles, like *Truly Flabby Preludes for a Dog* (1911). He worked with Cocteau on the ballet *Parade* (1917); its orchestral score included parts for typewriter and revolver. Though widely ridiculed, he tried to eliminate complexity and snobbery in 'serious' music, and he greatly influenced later composers.

Arnold Schoenberg (1874-1951)

One of the most revolutionary and influential 20th century composers, Schoenberg was born in Vienna. He had little formal musical education and taught himself theory and composition. His early works were reminiscent of Wagner and Strauss, but in 1908 he turned to an atonal style. He also developed a system of serialism, in which melodies and harmonies are derived from a row, or series, of all twelve chromatic tones. His best known works include *Pierrot lunaire* (1912), *Gurrelieder* for orchestra and chorus (begun in 1900) and the opera *Moses und Aront* 1930-2). In 1926, Schoenberg began teaching in Berlin, but with the Nazi rise to power in 1933, he emigrated to Los Angeles, where he continued to teach and compose until his death in 1951.

Edgard Varèse (1883-1965)

Varèse, a leading experimental composer of the 20th century, was born in Paris. His early years as a composer were spent in Paris and Berlin; he emigrated to America in 1915. His most renowned works are rhythmically complex; *Ionisation* (1930-3) was written entirely for thirteen percussion players. He experimented with electronic instruments as early as 1933; his *Poème électronique* (1957-8) is considered a major work in the field.

Bibliography

Crow, T., ed. *Bartók Studies*. Harmonie Park Press (Pinewood, 1976).

Gershwin, I. *Lyrics on Several Occasions*. Doubleday (New York, 1959).

Goldberg, I. *George Gershwin and New York*. Wynwood Press (New York, 1958).

Jablonski, E. *Gershwin: A Biography*. Doubleday (New York, 1987).

Jablonski, E. and L. Stewart. *The Gershwin Years*. Wynwood Press (New York, 1989).

Lendvai, E. *Béla Bartók: An Analysis of his Music*. Humanities (Atlantic Highlands, 1971).

Stravinsky, I. *Autobiography*. Norton (New York, 1962).

Stravinsky, I. and R. Craft. *Conversations with Igor Stravinsky*. University of California Press (Berkeley, 1980).

Stravinsky, I. *Themes and Conclusions*. University of California Press (Berkeley, 1982).

Suchoff, B. *Guide to Bartók*. Da Capo (New York, 1982).

Suchoff, B. *Bartók Mikrokosmos*. Martin (Los Angeles, 1976).

Vlad, R. *Stravinsky*. Oxford University Press (New York, 1979).

White, W. *Stravinsky*. University of California Press (Berkeley, 1980).

White, W. *Stravinsky: A Critical Survey*. Greenwood (Westport, 1979).

Index

Index

Contents

How to Use this Index

The following pages are a complete index to volumes 1 to 5 of Great Composers II: Their Lives and Times. The index consists of three sections: a General Index, an Index of Composers and an Index of Music.

The General Index

This index includes all topics – historical events, technical terms, countries, people, and, of course, music and composers – that appear in the five volumes. Where possible, people are indexed under surnames; where this is inappropriate (for example, Nicholas II, Tsar of Russia), the person is listed under his or her most familiar name. Works of art (paintings, books and plays) are also indexed in this section following the artist's name. For detailed entries on composers and on specific types or pieces of music, turn immediately to the Index of Composers or the Index of Music respectively.

The Index of Composers

In this section all composers appearing in the five volumes of Great Composers II: Their Lives and Times are listed with detailed subentries. Composers are listed under their best-known names – usually their main surname as in Falla, Maunel de or Rimsky-Korsakov, Nikolay – with their dates of birth and death following in parenthesis. The subentries beneath each composer's name detail his or her life and works, but specific pieces of music are listed in the Index of Music.

The Index of Music

All pieces of music referred to in this series are included in this index, not under their individual titles, but under their types – arias, concertos, oratorios, etc. Under these headings, composers are listed alphabetically by surname and their relevant works follow. There are also general entries on types of music.

Using the index

The number immediately following an entry is the number of the relevant volume. This is followed by a colon and then the page numbers on which the entry appears. If an entry can also be found in other volumes, these volumes and page numbers are printed in numerical order and are separated by a semi-colon. Page numbers which refer to illustrations are printed in italics in all three indexes, as are titles of books, paintings, and movies. Names of works of music – for example, Dvořák's Cello concerto in B minor – are not printed in italics unless they are titles of operas, songs, ballets or are general titles of groups of works – for example, Elgar's *Pomp and Circumstance* marches. The composers who are featured in the five volumes of this series are printed in bold type, both in the General Index and the Index of Composers.

General Index

Composer	Volume
Bartók	5
Debussy	1
Dvořák	2
Elgar	4
Gershwin	5
Grieg	2
Holst	4
Mussorgsky	3
Offenbach	1
Orff	5
Prokofiev	3
Rachmaninov	3
Ravel	1
Rimsky-Korsakov	3
Rodrigo	4
Shostakovich	3
Sibelius	2
Smetana	2
Strauss II, Johann	1
Strauss, Richard	4
Stravinsky	5

Kun, Béla 5:13, *14*
Kvapil (librettist) 2:41
Kyrillovna, Anna 5:36, *36*

L

'l'affaire Ravel' 1:91
l'Ecole Normale de Musique, Paris:
    Rodrigo at 4:*89*, 89-90
La Jeune France 1:99
LALO, Edouard *see* Index of Composers
LAMBERT, Constant *see* Index of
    Composers
Landsmål 2:81, *81*
Landstad, M. 2:81
Lanner, Josef 1:*36*, 45, 50
Larisch, Countess 1:57
Larrocha, Alicia de 4:97
Lasker, Vally 4:68
LASSUS, Roland de *see* Index
    of Composers
Lauret, Jeanette 1:19
Lavery, John 3:78
Lawrence, T. E. 3:80
Le Belvédère, Montfort L'Amaury 1:93, *94*
Le Mans, defeat of 1:29
Le Temps on *La Mer* 1:70
League of Nations, foundation of 2:32
LECOCQ, Alexandre Charles *see* Index of
    Composers
Lediard, Clara 4:62, *62*
Leeds Festival, Elgar and 4:12, 18
    Grieg and 2:69
Leete, Alfred, war poster 3:78
Legion of Honour, awarded to Bartók 5:11
LEHAR, Franz *see* Index of
    Composers
Leicester, Hubert 4:*11*
Leicester, William 4:*11*
Leipzig Conservatoire 2:*63*
    Elgar and 4:10
    Grieg at 2:63
Leipzig Symphony Orchestra and Chorus
    5:75
Leipzig: Elgar in 4:11
    Smetana in 2:13
Lenau, Nikolaus, and Strauss 4:47
Lenin, on the Paris Commune 1:31
Leningrad: siege of 3:92
    Stravinsky in 5:41
Leonova, Darya, and Mussorgsky 3:15
Leroy, Louis, and Impressionism 1:80
Levi, Hermann 4:36
Lewis, Wyndham 3:78
Lie, Jonas 2:83
Liehmann, Antonin, and Dvořák 2:38
Lifar, Serge 5:58
Lindbergh, Charles 5:82, *82*
Lindemann, Ludvig 2:81
    Older and Newer Mountain Melodies
    2:66, *67*
LISZT, Franz *see* Index of Composers
Litchfield County Choral Union 2:92
Liverpool Orchestral Society, Elgar and
    4:14
Livry, Emma 1:15
Llano, General Quiepode 4:105, 107
Lloyd-Weber, Julian, Rodrigo and 4:*92*, 93

Llubera, Lina 3:89, *89*
Lodizhensky, Anna 3:64
London School of Oriental Languages,
    Holst at 4:64
London Symphony Orchestra: Elgar and
    4:16, 17
London: 'Battle of Cable Street' 4:58
    Elgar in 4:10, 12, 15
        musical variations on 4:*13*
        returns to 4:16-17
    Gershwin in 5:90
    Holst in 4:66-7
    'Jetty' Treffz in 1:41
    Napoleon III in 1:26, *26*
    Offenbach in 1:14, 15
        concerts 1:11
    Prokofiev in 3:89
    Ravel in 1:94
    Rimsky-Korsakov in 3:37
    Strauss II in 1:41, 42
        Promenade Concerts 1:*40*, 41
Longfellow: *Hiawatha* 2:43
Lorca, Garcia 4:109
Louÿs, Pierre: and Debussy 1:64
    ends friendship with 1:65
    poems set to music by 1:75
Lower Rhine Festival, and Elgar 4:15
Lubbe, Marinus van der 4:51
Luccheni, Luigi 1:57
Ludendorff, General 4:54
Ludwig of Bavaria, 'Mad' King 1:55, *56*
Lumbye, Hans 1:50
Lunacharsky, Anatoly 3:87, 89
    Prokofiev and 3:94
Lusitania, sinking of the 3:84
lute 4:97
Luther, Martin, and music teaching 4:71
Luxemburg, Rosa 4:*54*, 56
LYADOV, Anatoli *see* Index of Composers
Lygon, Lady Mary 4:13, *24*
Lyknová, Barbora 2:10

M

Maazel, Lorin 1:75, *75*
Mack the Knife 5:99
MacMahon, General 1:*26*
madrigal, revival of 4:22
Maeterlinck, Maurice, Debussy's use of
    work by 1:65
MAHLER, Gustav *see* Index of Composers
Makievicz, Countess 4:84
Malevich 5:28-9
Mallarmé 1:62, 69
    Debussy and 1:69
        inspiration for 1:64
    Prélude à l'après-midi d'un faune 1:64,
    66
Malo-Yaroslavets restaurant, Moscow 3:14
Manchester School Composers *see* Index
    of Composers
Manet, Edouard 1:79
    anti-establishment stance 1:79-80
    and bullfights 1:106
    Dead Toreador 1:*107*
    Dejeuner sur l'herbe 1:79; 5:*24-25*
    influences on 1:64
        of Goya 1:106

Olympia 1:79
Mannhiem opera house, Orff and 5:64
Manns, August: concerts 4:11
    Elgar and 4:12
marches *see* Index of Music
Maria Teresa, Empress 2:24, *24*
Mariinsky Theatre, St Petersburg 5:51-2
    school 5:54
marionette theatre 5:63
    Orff and 5:62
Marmontov, Rachmaninov and 3:65
Marmoutel, Antoine, and Debussy 1:62
Marseillaise, La 2:97, *97*
MARTINŮ, Boluslav *see* Index of
    Composers
Marx, Kompositionslehre 2:88
Masaryk, Thomas 2:31, *31*, 32
Mason, Lowell 2:45
MASSENET, Jules *see* Index of Composers
Massine, Leonide 1:16, 19
    and *Gaieté Parisienne* score 1:18
    Stravinsky and 5:38
    and *The Rite of Spring* 5:45
Master of the King's Music 4:22
Matisse, Henri 5:*24*
Maud, Queen 2:84
Maupassant, The Five and 3:16
Maurice-Emmanuel, and Rodrigo 4:91
Mauté, Antoinette-Flore; and Debussy
    1:61-2
Mayer, Robert, children's concerts 4:71
Mayerling scandal 1:52-8
Mayr, Smetana and 2:13, 15
McCoy, Joseph 2:52
Meck, Nadezhda von, Debussy and 1:62
Medico-Surgical Academy, St Petersburg
    3:*12*
    Borodin at 3:12, *12*
Mehta, Zubin 4:75
Meiningen, Strauss in 4:36
melody, Debussy and 1:69
Mendelson, Mira 3:90
MENDELSSOHN, Felix *see* Index of
    Composers
Mensendieck Gymnastics 5:65
Menshikov, Prince 3:30
Menuhin, Yehudi 4:*17*
    commission for Bartók 5:15
Mercure de France, on *La Mer* 1:70
Meredith, George, Holst and 4:63

Composer	Volume
Bartók	5
Debussy	1
Dvořák	2
Elgar	4
Gershwin	5
Grieg	2
Holst	4
Mussorgsky	3
Offenbach	1
Orff	5
Prokofiev	3
Rachmaninov	3
Ravel	1
Rimsky-Korsakov	3
Rodrigo	4
Shostakovich	3
Sibelius	2
Smetana	2
Strauss II, Johann	1
Strauss, Richard	4
Stravinsky	5

Index of Composers

Composer	Volume
Bartók	5
Debussy	1
Dvořák	2
Elgar	4
Gershwin	5
Grieg	2
Holst	4
Mussorgsky	3
Offenbach	1
Orff	5
Prokofiev	3
Rachmaninov	3
Ravel	1
Rimsky-Korsakov	3
Rodrigo	4
Shostakovich	3
Sibelius	2
Smetana	2
Strauss II, Johann	1
Strauss, Richard	4
Stravinsky	5

Index of Music

Composer	Volume
Bartók	5
Debussy	1
Dvořák	2
Elgar	4
Gershwin	5
Grieg	2
Holst	4
Mussorgsky	3
Offenbach	1
Orff	5
Prokofiev	3
Rachmaninov	3
Ravel	1
Rimsky-Korsakov	3
Rodrigo	4
Shostakovich	3
Sibelius	2
Smetana	2
Strauss II, Johann	1
Strauss, Richard	4
Stravinsky	5

Composer	Volume
Bartók	5
Debussy	1
Dvořák	2
Elgar	4
Gershwin	5
Grieg	2
Holst	4
Mussorgsky	3
Offenbach	1
Orff	5
Prokofiev	3
Rachmaninov	3
Ravel	1
Rimsky-Korsakov	3
Rodrigo	4
Shostakovich	3
Sibelius	2
Smetana	2
Strauss II, Johann	1
Strauss, Richard	4
Stravinsky	5

W